NURSING HOME NEGLIGENCE

by
Margaret C. Jasper

Oceana's Legal Almanac Series
Law for the Layperson

2003
Oceana Publications, Inc.
Dobbs Ferry, New York

Information contained in this work has been obtained by Oceana Publications from sources believed to be reliable. However, neither the Publisher nor its authors guarantee the accuracy or completeness of any information published herein, and neither Oceana nor its authors shall be responsible for any errors, omissions or damages arising from the use of this information. This work is published with the understanding that Oceana and its authors are supplying information, but are not attempting to render legal or other professional services. If such services are required, the assistance of an appropriate professional should be sought.

You may order this or any Oceana publication by visiting Oceana's website at http://www.oceanalaw.com or contacting Customer Service at 1.914.693.8100 (domestic or international) or 1.800.831.0758 (U.S. only).

Library of Congress Control Number: 2003109090

ISBN: 0-379-11373-2

Oceana's Legal Almanac Series: Law for the Layperson
ISSN 1075-7376

Manufactured in the United States of America on acid-free paper.

To My Husband Chris

Your love and support
are my motivation and inspiration

-and-

In memory of my son, Jimmy

Table of Contents

ABOUT THE AUTHOR iii

INTRODUCTION v

CHAPTER 1:
OVERVIEW OF THE NURSING HOME SYSTEM

In General 1

Types of Nursing Homes. 1

Personal Care Nursing Facility. *1*

Medicaid Nursing Facility. *2*

Medicare Skilled Nursing Facility *2*

Costs and Coverage 2

Long-Term Health Care Insurance 2

Choosing a Long-Term Care Insurance Policy. *3*

Medicare 4

Medigap Insurance *4*

Medicaid 4

CHAPTER 2:
SELECTING A NURSING HOME

In General 7

Quality of Care 7

Medicare Nursing Home Compare Website. *7*

Long-Term Care Ombudsman *8*

The Joint Commission on Accreditation of Healthcare Organizations (JCAHO). . . *8*

Medicare/Medicaid Certification *9*

Visiting the Nursing Home 10

Considerations 10

The Admission Contract 11

Establishing A Care Plan 12

Monitoring the Nursing Home 13

Understaffing. 14

Ending the Nursing Home/Resident Relationship 14

CHAPTER 3:
LEGAL RIGHTS OF NURSING HOME RESIDENTS

In General 17

The Rights of Nursing Home Residents 17

The Right to be Free from Discrimination 17
The Right to be Treated Respectfully 18
The Right to be Free from Abuse and Neglect 18
The Right to be Free From Restraints 18
The Right to Receive Information on Services and Fees 18
The Right to Manage Money 18
The Right to Privacy 19
The Right to Joint Living Space for Married Couple 19
The Right to Medical Care 19
The Right to Visitors 19
The Right to Necessary Social Services 19
The Right to File Grievances 19
The Right to Remain in the Nursing Home 20
The Right to Leave the Nursing Home 20

The Nursing Home Reform Act of 1987 20

Care Requirements 21

Certification Surveys 22

Title VII of The Older Americans Act: Vulnerable
Elder Rights Protection 23

CHAPTER 4:
NURSING HOME NEGLECT

In General 25

Malnutrition and Dehydration 25
Pressure Sores 26
Falls 26
Wandering and Elopement 27

CHAPTER 5:
NURSING HOME ABUSE

In General 29

Physical Abuse 29
Sexual Abuse 30
Mental Abuse 31
Financial Abuse 31
Nursing Home Liability for Abuse 31
The National Center for Elder Abuse 32

CHAPTER 6:
REMEDIES

In General 33
Meeting with the Staff 33

The Family Council 33
Advocacy Groups. 34
  The Long-Term Care Ombudsman. *34*
Legal Services for the Elderly 34
State Licensing Agencies. 35
The Health Care Financing Administration 36
Litigation 36
  Medical Negligence *36*

APPENDICES

APPENDIX 1: NUMBER OF NURSING HOME RESIDENTS AGE 65 OR OLDER, BY AGE GROUP (1985-1995-1997-1999) (IN THOUSANDS). 39

APPENDIX 2: NUMBER OF MALE NURSING HOME RESIDENTS AGE 65 OR OLDER (1985-1995-1997-1999) (IN THOUSANDS) 41

APPENDIX 3: NUMBER OF FEMALE NURSING HOME RESIDENTS AGE 65 OR OLDER (1985-1995-1997-1999) (IN THOUSANDS) 43

APPENDIX 4: MEDICARE PATIENTS' STATEMENT OF RIGHTS. 45

APPENDIX 5: NURSING HOME NEEDS ASSESSMENT SURVEY. 47

APPENDIX 6: DIRECTORY OF STATE AGENCIES ON AGING 53

APPENDIX 7: DIRECTORY OF NATIONAL ORGANIZATIONS FOR THE ELDERLY. 59

APPENDIX 8 DIRECTORY OF STATE OFFICES OF LONG-TERM CARE OMBUDSMAN 63

APPENDIX 9: DIRECTORY OF STATE LICENSING AGENCIES FOR MEDICAL FACILITIES 67

APPENDIX 10: NURSING HOME CHECKLIST. 73

APPENDIX 11: THE FEDERAL NURSING HOME REFORM LAW (MEDICAID PROVISION) 79

APPENDIX 12: TITLE VII OF THE OLDER AMERICANS ACT: VULNERABLE ELDER RIGHTS PROTECTION. 129

APPENDIX 13: STATE STATUTES CONCERNING ELDER ABUSE 133

APPENDIX 14: DIRECTORY OF NATIONAL LEGAL SERVICES FOR THE ELDERLY. 139

GLOSSARY. 141

BIBLIOGRAPHY AND SUGGESTED READING. 151

ABOUT THE AUTHOR

MARGARET C. JASPER is an attorney engaged in the general practice of law in South Salem, New York, concentrating in the areas of personal injury and entertainment law. Ms. Jasper holds a Juris Doctor degree from Pace University School of Law, White Plains, New York, is a member of the New York and Connecticut bars, and is certified to practice before the United States District Courts for the Southern and Eastern Districts of New York, the United States Court of Appeals for the Second Circuit, and the United States Supreme Court.

Ms. Jasper has been appointed to the panel of arbitrators of the American Arbitration Association and the law guardian panel for the Family Court of the State of New York, is a member of the Association of Trial Lawyers of America, and is a New York State licensed real estate broker and member of the Westchester County Board of Realtors, operating as Jasper Real Estate, in South Salem, New York. Margaret Jasper maintains a website at http://www.JasperLawOffice.com.

Ms. Jasper is the author and general editor of the following legal almanacs: AIDS Law; The Americans with Disabilities Act; Animal Rights Law; The Law of Attachment and Garnishment; Bankruptcy Law for the Individual Debtor; Individual Bankruptcy and Restructuring; Banks and their Customers; The Law of Buying and Selling; The Law of Capital Punishment; The Law of Child Custody; Commercial Law; Consumer Rights Law; The Law of Contracts; Copyright Law; Credit Cards and the Law; The Law of Debt Collection; Dictionary of Selected Legal Terms; The Law of Dispute Resolution; The Law of Drunk Driving; Education Law; Elder Law; Employee Rights in the Workplace; Employment Discrimination Under Title VII; Environmental Law; Estate Planning; Everyday Legal Forms; Executors and Personal Representatives: Rights and Responsibilities; Harassment in the Workplace; Health Care and Your Rights. Home Mortgage Law Primer; Hospital Liability Law; Identity Theft and How To Protect Yourself; Insurance Law; International Adoption; The Law of Immigration; Juvenile Justice and Children's Law; Labor Law; Landlord-Tenant Law; The Law of Libel and Slander; Marriage and Divorce; The Law of Medical Malpractice;

Motor Vehicle Law; The Law of No-Fault Insurance; The Law of Obscenity and Pornography; Patent Law; The Law of Personal Injury; Probate Law; The Law of Product Liability; Real Estate Law for the Homeowner and Broker; Religion and the Law; The Right to Die; Law for the Small Business Owner; Social Security Law; Special Education Law; The Law of Speech and the First Amendment; Teenagers and Substance Abuse; Trademark Law; Victim's Rights Law; The Law of Violence Against Women; Welfare: Your Rights and the Law; and Workers' Compensation Law.

INTRODUCTION

Approximately one and a half million elderly and disabled adults presently reside in nursing homes in the United States. Depending on the level of care needed by the individual, nursing homes offer varying levels of care. For example, many nursing homes are merely residential facilities which provide room and board, and general assistance with daily activities for the residents. There are no medical services available.

A higher level of care is offered in a facility known as a skilled nursing home. A skilled nursing home provides health care to its residents, who are likely in need of special medical services. A skilled nursing home also employs health care providers, such as nurses, to attend to the residents.

Unfortunately, abuse and neglect in the nursing home setting has become a widespread problem. There have been reports of serious injuries and deaths of many helpless nursing home residents, who are often left to needlessly suffer. This is due, in large part, to the lack of credentials required of nursing home employees, as well as the problem of understaffing. In addition, many nursing home employees have no training, are underpaid and overworked.

If a resident sustains injuries in a non-skilled nursing home, or suffers physical neglect, the nursing home would likely be liable for general negligence as opposed to medical malpractice. In a skilled nursing home, liability may occur if a health care provider rendered negligent medical care to a resident.

The most likely medical malpractice claim to arise in a nursing home would include medical neglect, e.g., a lack of care for existing medical problems of a resident. This could include, for example, failure to prevent dehydration and malnutrition; negligence in providing medication and failure to provide reasonable access to medical services, etc.

In order to reduce the possibility of any type of negligence in the nursing home setting, family members should investigate the background of the home and its staff, including the staff to resident ratio. If it is a skilled nursing home, one should also inquire into the credentials and training of the medical staff, such as the nursing staff, to determine whether they are trained in the area of the prospective resident's diagnosis.

For example, if a family member is suffering from Alzheimer's Disease, determine whether the medical staff at the nursing home has experience working with such patients. In addition, find out the ratio of nurses to residents, and the level of need required by the other residents, to ensure that there is adequate medical coverage.

This almanac presents an overview of the nursing home system in America, including the types of nursing homes, the level of care offered, and information on selecting an appropriate facility. This almanac also explores the problem of nursing home negligence and abuse, the types of neglect and abuse, and the ways to recognize and address these problems. The legislation developed to prevent nursing home neglect and abuse is also discussed, including the legal rights of the nursing home resident, and the remedies available under the law.

The Appendix provides resource directories, applicable statutes, and other pertinent information and data. The Glossary contains definitions of many of the terms used throughout the almanac.

CHAPTER 1:
OVERVIEW OF THE NURSING HOME SYSTEM

IN GENERAL

Unfortunately, many Americans have health care problems which render them disabled and dependent on others to help them with their daily activities. In fact, over one and a half million elderly and disabled adults presently reside in nursing homes in America.

Tables setting forth the number of nursing home residents by age and gender are set forth at Appendices 1, 2 and 3 of this almanac.

Unlike acute care—short-term, recuperative care provided by a hospital—long-term care is the type of care given to a person who has become disabled or who suffers from a chronic illness. In such a case, important decisions must be made about the proper setting in which such care may be given.

A nursing home generally refers to a residential facility that provides shelter and care for senior citizens and other disabled individuals who are unable to live independently. As discussed below, these facilities offer varying levels of care, depending on the needs of the resident.

TYPES OF NURSING HOMES

In general, there are three types of nursing homes:

Personal Care Nursing Facility

A Personal Care Nursing Facility provides the senior citizen who does not need any special medical care with room and board and basic assistance with daily activities. These long-term care facilities are generally not covered by Medicare and Medicaid primarily because of the lack of significant medical care needed by the residents.

Medicaid Nursing Facility

A Medicaid Nursing Facility provides the senior citizen or disabled individual with a limited range of skilled nursing care, rehabilitation services, and other necessary health-related care. Medicare does not pay for residence in such facilities, however Medicaid may reimburse the costs of such care provided a doctor certifies that the resident is in need of this level of care. Further, the resident must meet certain financial guidelines to qualify for admission.

Medicare Skilled Nursing Facility

A Medicare Skilled Nursing Facility provides the senior citizen or disabled individual with the most highly skilled nursing care available outside of a hospital setting, including many specialized services. Medicare pays up to 150 days per calendar year for residence at such a facility, provided the resident's physician certifies that they are in need of such a high level of care.

COSTS AND COVERAGE

Unfortunately, nursing home care is extremely expensive, and is rarely covered by private health insurance. The average cost of care in a nursing home is estimated at $40,000 per year and more, depending on the facility, the location, and the level of care provided. Most nursing homes charge a basic fee for room, meals, and some personal care, and the resident may have to pay extra for other services or care for special medical needs.

Most people who enter a nursing home begin by paying for their nursing home care by using their personal resources. The majority of the cost of this care is borne by the patients and their families. This is particularly burdensome in the retirement years when most older persons are on fixed incomes.

As discussed below, some senior citizens may be covered under long-term care insurance. Although Medicare covers some skilled nursing and rehabilitative care, it generally does not cover general custodial care, e.g., help with activities of daily living, like bathing, dressing, and using the bathroom. Medicaid presently pays for the care of most—7 out of 10—nursing home residents.

Long-Term Health Care Insurance

Responding to the need for financial assistance in the event long-term care becomes necessary, a number of insurance companies have stepped in to fill the gap, providing a variety of insurance policies covering long-term care. If one is considering purchasing such a policy, it would be prudent to review the benefits being offered by the various companies in order to choose the policy that best fits your needs.

Although long-term care insurance can be very helpful if it is ever needed, it can also be quite costly, ranging anywhere from $250 to over $2000 per year for the average senior citizen who is in good health. Before taking on this considerable expense, it would be wise to carefully assess one's individual situation and investigate all resources available from other programs. Some of the factors one should consider when assessing the need for long-term care insurance include:

1. The individual's present financial situation and projected financial situation following retirement.

2. The individual's ability to afford long-term care insurance.

3. The programs the individual expects to be eligible for upon retirement and whether they will be able to meet his or her needs.

4. The likelihood that the individual will require long-term care in the future, based on his or her present health and family history.

5. The alternative resources the individual expects to have if long-term care is needed, such as family and friends, and the availability of community-based services.

Choosing a Long-Term Care Insurance Policy

Since long-term care insurance is a fairly recent development, one must be very careful in selecting and evaluating the various policies available, and inquiring into the background and stability of the companies offering such insurance. In addition, every policy generally contains some restrictions and limitations.

Long-term care insurance policies typically cover nursing home care. Some policies cover all levels of nursing home care—skilled nursing care, intermediate care, and custodial care—while others may cover only a certain level of care, such as skilled nursing care. It is best to purchase a policy that covers all levels of nursing home care, since long-term skilled nursing care is not usually needed. It is more likely that a person will need a lesser level of nursing home care, such as custodial care, over an extended period of time.

Most policies pay only a preset daily benefit for nursing home care or home health care, and the difference between the amount covered by the insurance and the actual costs of care is borne by the insured. Some policies allow the insured to pay higher premiums in return for higher daily benefits. Generally, policies that provide for a longer duration of care and benefits will be more costly.

Medicare

Medicare is a federal health insurance program administered by the Social Security Administration (SSA), designated for seniors and people with disabilities, regardless of income. Medicare is an entitlement program funded by payroll taxes. When a person reaches age 65, he or she usually becomes eligible for Medicare. Unfortunately, Medicare does not cover non-skilled custodial nursing home care.

There are two parts to the Medicare policy: (i) Part A Hospitalization Coverage; and (ii) Part B Medical Coverage. Under Part A, a Medicare recipient is entitled to 100 days of care in a Medicare-certified skilled nursing facility per benefit period, provided: (i) the patient was hospitalized for at least three days during the 30 days prior to admission; and (ii) the patient needs and receives daily skilled services.

Medicare defines "daily" as seven days a week of skilled nursing and five days a week of skilled therapy. Skilled nursing and therapy services include evaluation and management as well as observation and assessment of a patient's condition. Medicare pays for the first 20 days in full. For days 21 through 100, the patient pays a portion of the costs.

The Medicare Patient's Statement of Rights is set forth at Appendix 4.

Medigap Insurance

Eligible Medicare recipients may also purchase supplemental coverage known as Medigap insurance. Medigap policies generally pay for medical-related expenses not reimbursed by Medicare, such as hospital deductibles and co-payments. Although Medigap policies are designed to supplement Medicare, they usually do not cover general long-term custodial care. However, some policies do provide for skilled nursing home care. Nevertheless, if Medicare refuses to cover medical care because it is unreasonable and unnecessary, Medigap will not cover it either.

Medicaid

The Medicaid program was established in 1965 as an amendment to the Social Security Act of 1935 and was administered by the Social Security Administration until 1977. In 1977, administration of the Medicaid program was transferred to the Department of Health and Human Services and to the Health Care Financing Administration. The Medicaid program continued to be administered by the Health Care Financing Administration until June 2001, when the agency was renamed the Centers for Medicare and Medicaid Services (CMS).

Medicaid is jointly financed and administered by the federal and state governments as the primary source of health care coverage for low-income individuals, as well as the blind and disabled populations in America. Medicaid is the primary public provider for home health and nursing home care.

Each state has its own rules concerning eligibility and coverage, which may be complex, therefore, the reader is advised to check the law of his or her own jurisdiction for specific rules.

Medicare recipients who have low income and limited resources may receive help paying their out-of-pocket medical expenses from their state's Medicaid program. This is generally referred to as "dual eligibility." Services that are covered by both programs are paid first by Medicare, and the difference is paid by Medicaid, up to the state's designated limit. Medicaid also covers nursing home care beyond the time period covered by Medicare.

When long-term care is unavoidable, Congress gave the states the option to use a special income rule to provide Medicaid to persons in nursing homes who have too much income to qualify for Supplemental Security Income (SSI) benefits, but not enough income to cover their expensive long-term care. In addition, the states must allow nursing facility residents to retain a small amount of their income as an allowance for personal items.

CHAPTER 2:
SELECTING A NURSING HOME

IN GENERAL

Choosing a nursing home is a very important decision. A nursing home provides care to people who cannot be cared for at home due to physical, emotional, or mental problems. Nursing homes can provide a wide range of personal care and health services. For many people, this care generally is considered custodial—i.e. non-skilled—care. The first step in selecting a nursing home is to determine the level of care needed.

A nursing home needs assessment survey is set forth at Appendix 5 of this almanac.

QUALITY OF CARE

It is important to make sure that the nursing home selected offers quality care to its residents. Nursing homes are certified to make sure they meet certain Federal health and safety requirements. In making long-term care choices, one should ask trusted friends and relatives who may be familiar with the area nursing homes. It may also be helpful to contact one of the many agencies dedicated to assisting senior citizens.

A directory of state agencies on aging is set forth at Appendix 6 of this almanac, and a directory of national organizations for the elderly is set forth at Appendix 7 of this almanac.

Medicare Nursing Home Compare Website

A comparison of nursing homes in one's area can be made by going to the "Nursing Home Compare" page of the Medicare website (www.medicare.gov). At this website, one can review the state inspection reports of the nursing homes in their area, as well as resident characteristics and staffing levels. The service has information about nursing homes in all 50 states, the District of Columbia, and some U.S. territories.

Information contained on the website includes:

1. The percentage of residents with loss of ability in basic daily tasks since their need for help was last assessed, including:

(a) feeding oneself;

(b) moving from one chair to another;

(c) changing positions while in bed; and

(d) going to the bathroom alone.

2. The petcentage of residents with pressure sores, commonly referred to as bedsores.

3. The percentage of residents with bad or moderate enduring pain.

4. The percentage of residents with infections, including pneumonia, wound infections, urinary tract or a bladder infections.

5. The percentage of residents in physical restraints.

6. The percentage of short-stay residents—i.e., residents who stay for less than 90 days.

7. The percentage of short-stay residents with pain.

8. The percentage of short-stay residents with delirium.

Long-Term Care Ombudsman

Another way of determining quality of care is by contacting the state office of Long-Term Care Ombudsman. The Ombudsman program is a very good source of general information about nursing homes. Ombudsmen visit nursing homes and speak with residents throughout the year to make sure residents' rights are protected. They also work to solve problems a resident may have with their nursing home care, including quality of care and financial issues.

The Ombudsman program may be able to share information concerning the number and type of complaints they have received about a particular nursing home, and how those problems were resolved.

A directory of state offices of the Long-Term Care Ombudsman is set forth at Appendix 8 of this almanac.

The Joint Commission on Accreditation of Healthcare Organizations (JCAHO)

The Joint Commission on Accreditation of Healthcare Organizations (JCAHO) is the nation's predominant standards-setting and accrediting body in health care and evaluates and accredits nearly 19,000 health care organizations and programs in the United States. The JCAHO was founded in 1951 as an independent, not-for-profit organization. The mission of the JCAHO is to continuously improve the safety and quality of care provided to the public through the provision of health care accreditation and related services that support performance improvement in health care organizations.

The JCAHO evaluation and accreditation services are provided for a number of medical facilities, including nursing homes and other long term care facilities. Accreditation by the JCAHO is recognized nationwide as a symbol of quality that indicates that an organization meets certain performance standards.

The JCAHO's standards address the organization's level of performance in key functional areas, such as patient rights. The JCAHO develops its standards in consultation with health care experts, providers, measurement experts, purchasers and consumers. To earn and maintain accreditation, an organization must undergo an on-site survey by a JCAHO survey team at least every three years.

The JCAHO also publishes "Quality Check"—a comprehensive internet guide to accredited organizations. Quality Check provides a searchable database of nearly 20,000 JCAHO-accredited health care organizations and programs throughout the United States and includes each organization's name, address, telephone number, accreditation decision, accreditation date, and current accreditation status and effective date.

In addition, for more in-depth quality information, consumers can check the individual performance reports available for many accredited organizations. Performance reports provide detailed information about an organization's performance and how it compares to similar organizations.

Medicare/Medicaid Certification

It is important to find out whether the nursing home is Medicare/Medicaid certified. This means the nursing home has passed an inspection survey done by a state government agency. Medicare and Medicaid will only pay for care in a certified nursing home. In addition, make sure the nursing home, nursing staff and administrator are properly licensed.

A directory of state licensing agencies for medical facilities is set forth at Appendix 9.

VISITING THE NURSING HOME

Before selecting a nursing home, it is important to visit the facility. A visit gives you the chance to see and speak with the residents and staff, and view the facility and accommodations. When you visit the nursing home, it is important to bring a checklist so that you do not forget to ask any important questions. This checklist has questions about basic information, resident appearance, nursing home living spaces, staff, residents' rooms, hallways, stairs, lounges, bathrooms, menus and food, activities, and safety and care.

A nursing home checklist prepared by the Centers for Medicare and Medicaid Services is set forth at Appendix 10.

Also ask for a copy of the nursing home's inspection report. The inspection report tells you how well the nursing home meets Federal health and safety requirements. The nursing home is required to maintain and make available the results of the most recent survey undertaken of the facility by Federal or State surveyors.

You should also make arrangements to revisit the nursing home on another weekday and/or weekend, and at a different time of day to compare the atmosphere and activities, and meet additional members of the staff who may not have been on duty during your first visit.

Nursing homes also hold "council" meetings among the staff, residents and family members. Ask for permission to attend one of the council meetings so you can assess the opinion of the current residents and family members.

If you are uncomfortable about anything you see, or anyone you meet, at a particular nursing home, you may want to trust your instincts and choose another nursing home. If, however, it appears that the facility is clean and well-kept, the residents seem comfortable and treated well, and the staff is friendly and available, that can help in making a good decision.

CONSIDERATIONS

Some of the things one may consider when selecting a nursing home that meets their needs, are as follows:

1. How does the staff treat the residents?

2. What kind of recreational activities are available?

3. What kind of religious services are available?

4. Can the residents decorate their rooms?

5. What level of privacy is afforded residents?

6. What is the ratio of staff to residents?

7. What are the medical arrangements?

8. Does the nursing home arrange for preventive care, such as routine checkups, flu and pneumonia shots?

9. Is a doctor available if necessary, and does the nursing home have an arrangement with an area hospital?

10. Were there any quality concerns as evidenced by the most recent inspection report?

11. What is the proximity of the nursing home to friends and family?

12. How frequent can friends and family members visit?

13. Are there any restrictions on visitation?

14. For communication purposes, is the resident's primary language spoken by the staff?

15. What services does the nursing home provide and what, if any, are the fees?

16. How does the nursing home manage the personal needs accounts of its residents?

17. Is the nursing home secure?

18. Is the nursing home accredited by the Joint Commission on the Accreditation of Healthcare Organizations (JCAHO)?

19. Is the nursing home a Medicare/Medicaid certified facility?

20. Is the nursing home, nursing staff and administrator licensed by the state?

21. Is the nursing home disabled friendly, e.g. are there wheelchair ramps for easy access, handrails in the hallways and grab bars in the bathroom?

22. Does the nursing home have an elevator if there are multiple floors?

23. Is the nursing home well-lit, and are there call bells strategically placed?

24. Are there smoke detectors and fire extinguishers?

THE ADMISSION CONTRACT

The admission contract is a written document that the resident will be asked to sign upon admission to the nursing home. The admission contract sets forth the resident's rights and the services the nursing home will provide in exchange for the fees it receives. The admission contract is a legally binding document.

Therefore, it is important to carefully review the admission contract to make sure the resident's rights are clearly spelled out, and that there are no misrepresentations. Pay particular attention to any provisions in the admission contract that limit the nursing home's liability if the resident is injured, or has property missing. In addition, the admission contract should not restrict visiting hours.

It is helpful to request a copy of the admission contract prior to the date of admission. This gives the resident and family members time to carefully review the document, ask questions, and get input from agencies who are familiar with nursing home contracts.

The admission contract is made with the resident, not a family member. Generally, the resident signs the contract. If the resident is incapable of signing the document, a family member with a power of attorney may sign the admission contract on the resident's behalf, as the agent of the resident. However, a nursing home cannot require a family member or friend to sign the admission contract as a "guarantor" or "responsible party" unless that person intends to pay for the resident's care. Imposing personal liability for the cost of the resident's care is illegal for residents receiving Medicaid.

ESTABLISHING A CARE PLAN

Upon admission to the nursing home, a care plan must be established in order to make sure that all of the resident's needs are met. Important information that should be included in the patient records includes:

1. The resident's medical insurance information, including the name of the insurance company and the policy number.

2. The resident's medical history, including past illnesses, treatments, operations, allergies, immunizations, etc.

3. The resident's current health status, including present health problems and any limitations on activities.

4. A list of the resident's current medications, including the name, purpose, and dosage, etc.

5. A list of the resident's health care providers, including names, addresses and telephone numbers, and specialties.

6. Information concerning the resident's advance health care directives, including whether the resident has executed (a) a durable power

of attorney for health care—a legal document that names someone to make health care decisions for the resident if they become unable to make their own decisions; and (b) a living will—a legal document that states what type of treatments the resident wants or does not want in case they are unable to convey their wishes.

7. A list of family members in case of emergency, including names, relationship to resident, addresses and telephone numbers.

In general, an initial health assessment must be conducted within 14 days of the resident's admission to the facility. Additional health assessments should be conducted at 90 day intervals unless the resident's medical condition requires more frequent checkups.

Depending on the resident's medical assessment, the health care plan may also detail the frequency and nature of any personal or health care services needed, such as physical therapy; any equipment or supplies needed, such as a wheelchair; and any special dietary information.

MONITORING THE NURSING HOME

If your loved one is residing in a nursing home, the best way to monitor how he or she is being treated is to make yourself visible. Make frequent visits to the facility to speak with the staff. Show up at different times of the day, and on different days, so that the staff is not prepared for your visit. Join the family council and attend the meetings. Demonstrate your knowledge of the applicable state and federal laws and regulations.

If your family member is in ill health and needs specialized attention, it is even more crucial that you become involved, and be alert to potential problems. If your family member needs assistance in feeding and drinking, it is especially important to make sure these needs are being taken care of because dehydration and malnutrition are serious problems in nursing homes, and can lead to life-threatening diseases and death.

Take time to visit the nursing home around mealtime. Make sure that the food is nutritious, balanced and served warm, and that drinks are readily available. If your family member is unable to self-feed, make sure that staff members are taking their time in feeding him or her. This takes patience.

During your visits, watch for the following signs of neglect:

1. Lack of assistance with feeding those residents who cannot feed themselves.

2. Lack of respect for the residents, such as harsh or disrespectful language.

3. Lack of privacy, e.g., residents should be clothed when in the common areas, and should be able to expect privacy when they are in their own rooms or in the bathroom.

4. Strong offensive odors, such as the smell of urine or feces, may indicate that there are not enough people on staff to attend to all of the residents' personal needs, or to maintain the cleanliness of the nursing home.

5. The use of restraints is humiliating, can be dangerous if not properly monitored, and may indicate that the nursing home is not able to attend to the safety of all of the residents in a more respectful manner.

6. Many unanswered call bells may be another indication that there are not enough staff members to attend to the needs of the residents.

UNDERSTAFFING

Understaffing is a major problem in nursing homes. Understaffing is a serious problem which can lead to the neglect and abuse of nursing home residents. According to a July 27, 2000 report by the U.S. Senate Special Committee on Aging, understaffing is directly linked to poor nursing home care, which is in turn linked to the increased hospitalization of nursing home residents.

More than one-half of American nursing homes are below the suggested minimum staffing level for nurse's aides, and more than one-third of nursing homes fell below the suggested minimum staffing level for registered nurses. Of total licensed staff, nearly one-fourth of all nursing homes fell below the suggested minimum staffing level.

As set forth in Chapter 3, state and Federal laws require that nursing homes which receive federal funds must maintain a sufficient number of employees to care for the residents.

Therefore, it is important to keep track of the ratio of staff to residents. If it is a high number, it is impossible to make sure all of the residents' needs are properly being met. Therefore, you should visit as much as possible to make sure your loved one is eating and drinking properly, and that their personal hygiene is properly maintained, to avoid serious illness.

ENDING THE NURSING HOME/RESIDENT RELATIONSHIP

The law permits a nursing home to end the resident's stay under the following conditions;

1. The nursing home is unable to meet the needs of the resident.

2. The resident's health has improved and he or she no longer needs the services of the nursing home.

3. The resident's presence in the nursing home is endangering the safety and/or health of other individuals.

4. Non-payment.

5. The nursing home is closing down.

The resident is also entitled to leave the nursing home if they are dissatisfied or uncomfortable. However, it is important to first check with the nursing home about whether there are rules for leaving, in which case the nursing home may require the resident to pay an extra fee.

CHAPTER 3:
LEGAL RIGHTS OF NURSING HOME RESIDENTS

IN GENERAL

State and Federal law provides certain rights and protections to nursing home residents. It is important for the resident and his or her family members to familiarize themselves with the Federal and state laws concerning the nursing home resident's rights. The nursing home is required to post these rights in the facility, and provide the resident with a written description of these legal rights.

Nursing homes that receive federal funding are required to comply with the federal laws that guarantee a high level of care to nursing home residents. In addition to federal laws regulating the quality of care in nursing homes, states have enacted laws as well. State laws may vary, therefore, the reader is advised to check the law of his or her own jurisdiction. The rights under state law must, however, compare with, or exceed, the rights provided under federal law. In fact, some states have adopted laws that are tougher than the federal laws.

Any violation of a resident's rights should be reported to the nursing home, following the established grievance procedures. If the problem is not addressed and corrected, the violation should be reported to the local long-term care ombudsman.

THE RIGHTS OF NURSING HOME RESIDENTS

The Right to be Free from Discrimination

Nursing homes do not have to accept all applicants, but they must comply with Civil Rights laws that do not allow discrimination based on race, color, national origin, disability, age, or religion under certain conditions.

The Right to be Treated Respectfully

A nursing home resident has the right to be treated with dignity and respect. The resident has the right to make their own schedule, including when they sleep, when they wake, and when they eat. They can choose which activities they want to engage in, and which they want to avoid. The only exception is that the resident's choice must conform to their plan of care.

The Right to be Free from Abuse and Neglect

A nursing home resident has the right to be free from verbal, sexual, physical, and mental abuse, and involuntary seclusion by anyone, including but not limited to nursing home staff, other residents, consultants, volunteers, staff from other agencies, family members or legal guardians, friends, or other individuals.

The Right to be Free From Restraints

A nursing home resident has the right to be free from physical or chemical restraints. Physical restraints include any manual method, or physical or mechanical device, material, or equipment attached to or near a person's body so that they can't remove the restraint easily. The restraint prevents freedom of movement or normal access to one's own body. A chemical restraint is a drug used to limit freedom of movement and is not needed to treat the person's medical symptoms.

It is against the law for a nursing home to use physical or chemical restraints, unless it is necessary to treat the resident's medical symptoms. For example, restraints may not be used to punish the resident, nor can a restraint be used for the convenience of nursing home staff. The resident has the right to refuse the use of restraints. The only exception is if the resident is at risk of harming himself or another.

The Right to Receive Information on Services and Fees

A nursing home resident must be informed, in writing, about services and fees before they move into the nursing home. In addition, the nursing home cannot require a minimum entrance fee.

The Right to Manage Money

A nursing home resident has the right to manage their own money or to choose someone they trust to manage their money. If the resident wants the nursing home to manage their personal funds, they must sign a written statement giving the nursing home permission to do so. The nursing home must protect the resident's funds from loss by buying a bond or some other type of protection method. In addition, the nursing home must provide the resident with access to their financial records, bank account, and cash reserve.

The Right to Privacy

A nursing home resident has the right to privacy. This includes the right to make telephone calls in private. In addition, the nursing home resident is entitled to keep their own personal property. Nevertheless, the nursing home is obligated to protect the resident's property from theft, e.g., by providing locked cabinets in the rooms. Nursing home staff is not permitted to open a resident's mail unless authorized by the resident.

The Right to Joint Living Space for Married Couple

If married residents are living in the same nursing home, they are entitled to share a room.

The Right to Medical Care

A nursing home resident has the right to be informed about their medical condition and any medications they are given. A resident also has the right to refuse any medication or treatment. The resident has the right to take part in developing their care plan, and must be given access to their medical records upon request. In addition, a resident has the right to see their own doctor.

The Right to Visitors

A nursing home resident has the right to spend private time with visitors, including those providing medical or legal services, at any reasonable hour. In addition, the nursing home must permit family members to visit the resident at any time. Conversely, the resident has the right to refuse to see any visitor.

The Right to Necessary Social Services

A nursing home resident has the right to necessary social services, including but not limited to counseling, legal assistance, and discharge coordination.

The Right to File Grievances

A nursing home resident has the right to complain without fear of reprisal. The nursing home is obligated to promptly address and resolve the resident's complaint.

The Right to Remain in the Nursing Home

A nursing home resident has the right to remain in the nursing home. He or she cannot be discharged or transferred to another facility unless:

1. Discharge or transfer is necessary for the health, welfare or safety of the resident or others.

2. The resident's health has declined to the point that the nursing home cannot meet their care needs.

3. The resident's health has improved to the point that nursing home care is no longer necessary.

4. The resident has not paid for its services.

5. The nursing home closes down.

Unless there is an emergency, the nursing home is required to give the resident 30 days advance notice of any plan to discharge or transfer the resident. The resident has the right to appeal this decision. Nevertheless, a nursing home cannot make a resident leave if they are waiting to obtain Medicaid.

If the resident is transferred to a hospital for treatment, the nursing home must give the resident written notice of how long it will hold the resident's bed open. This is called a "bedhold period." Once the bedhold period expires, if the resident is still hospitalized, the resident must be readmitted to the nursing home as soon as a bed becomes available.

The Right to Leave the Nursing Home

A nursing home has the right to leave the facility to visit with friends and family. A nursing home resident also has the right to leave the home and move to another facility. However, if the resident does not give the nursing home prior notice before leaving, the resident may incur an extra fee.

THE NURSING HOME REFORM ACT OF 1987

The primary piece of federal legislation aimed at ending the widespread neglect and abuse found in nursing homes during the 1980's is the Nursing Home Reform Act. Congress enacted this piece of legislation as part of the Omnibus Budget Reconciliation Act of 1987, in an effort to reform nursing home regulations and force compliance by any nursing home that participates in the Medicare and Medicaid programs. As described below, both the Medicare and Medicaid provisions of the law are practically identical.

The text of the Nursing Home Reform Act (Medicaid Provision) is set forth at Appendix 11.

Care Requirements

To participate in the Medicare and Medicaid programs, nursing homes must be in compliance with the federal requirements for long-term care as prescribed in the U.S. Code of Federal Regulations. Under the regulations, the nursing home must do the following:

1. The nursing home must have a sufficient nursing staff to provide nursing and related services to attain or maintain the highest practicable physical, mental, and psychosocial well-being of each resident, as determined by resident assessments and individual plans of care;

2. Within 14 days after admission, the nursing home must conduct a comprehensive, accurate, standardized, reproducible assessment of each resident's functional capacity, which must be regularly updated;

3. Within 7 days of the initial assessment, the nursing home must develop a comprehensive care plan that includes measurable objectives and timetables to meet a resident's medical, nursing, and mental and psychosocial needs that are identified in his or her comprehensive assessment, which must be regularly updated;

4. The nursing home must prevent the deterioration of a resident's ability to bathe, dress, groom, transfer and ambulate, toilet, eat, and to use speech, language or other functional communication systems;

5. The nursing home must provide the necessary services to maintain good nutrition, grooming, and personal and oral hygiene for those residents who are unable to carry out activities of daily living;

6. The nursing home must ensure that residents receive proper treatment and devices to maintain vision and hearing abilities;

7. The nursing home must ensure that residents do not develop pressure sores and, if a resident does develop pressure sores, the nursing home must provide the necessary treatment and services to promote healing, prevent infection and prevent new sores from developing;

8. The nursing home must provide appropriate treatment and services to incontinent residents to restore as much normal bladder functioning as possible and prevent urinary tract infections;

9. The nursing home must ensure that the resident receives adequate supervision and devices to prevent accidents;

10. The nursing home must ensure that the resident achieves acceptable nutritional status, such as body weight and protein level;

11. The nursing home must provide each resident with sufficient fluid intake to maintain proper hydration and health;

12. The nursing home must ensure that residents are free of any significant medication errors;

13. The nursing home must care for its residents in a manner and in an environment that promotes maintenance or enhancement of each resident's quality of life;

14. The nursing home must promote care for residents in a manner and in an environment that maintains or enhances each resident's dignity and respect in full recognition of his or her individuality;

15. The nursing home must ensure that the resident has the right to choose activities, schedules, and health care consistent with his or her interests, assessments and plan of care;

16. The nursing home must ensure that the medical care of each resident is supervised by a physician and must provide or arrange for the provision of physician services 24 hours a day, in case of an emergency;

17. The nursing home must provide pharmaceutical services to meet the needs of each resident; and

18. The nursing home must maintain clinical records on each resident in accordance with accepted professional standards and practices that are complete, accurately documented, readily accessible, and systematically organized.

CERTIFICATION SURVEYS

Under the law, nursing homes that are participating in the Medicaid and Medicare programs, are required to undergo an annual survey and certification process. The purpose of the survey process is to assess whether the quality of care, as intended by the law and regulations, and as needed by the resident, is actually being provided in nursing homes.

In order to remain certified, nursing homes must be in substantial compliance with the Medicaid and Medicare care requirements as well as state law. If a nursing home is found to be out of compliance, federal law sets forth enforcement options such as denial of payment for new admissions, civil money penalties, revocation of Medicaid and Medicare certifications, transfer of residents and the imposition of temporary management.

If the nursing home fails to meet a federal regulation, a deficiency is issued. Nevertheless, a 1999 U.S. Government study found that one-fourth of nursing homes nationwide continued to be cited for deficiencies that either caused actual harm to residents. or created the potential for death or serious injury.

TITLE VII OF THE OLDER AMERICANS ACT: VULNERABLE ELDER RIGHTS PROTECTION

The Older Americans Act was signed into law by President Johnson on July 14, 1965. In addition to creating the Administration on Aging, it authorized grants to States for community planning and services programs, as well as for research, demonstration and training projects in the field of aging. A 1992 amendment to the Act added, among other things, Title VII: Vulnerable Elder Rights Protection—a provision to protect and enhance the basic rights and benefits of vulnerable older people.

Title VII also includes provisions for long-term care ombudsman programs and state legal assistance development, and strengthens the programs for the prevention of abuse and exploitation. Title VII is designed to serve as an advocacy tool. In 2001, long-term ombudsmen investigated 264,269 thousand complaints against nursing homes and other adult care facilities.

The text of Title VII of the Older Americans Act concerning Vulnerable Elder Rights Protection is set forth at Appendix 12.

CHAPTER 4:
NURSING HOME NEGLECT

IN GENERAL

A large portion of the American population presently lives in nursing homes. Unfortunately, many of these nursing homes are understaffed, and the employees are usually underpaid and lack adequate training for the difficult tasks involved in taking care of elderly residents, who are often unable to attend to their basic daily needs. This scenario often leads to neglect, and needless pain and injury to the residents. The residents' health, welfare and safety are placed in jeopardy. This chapter discusses some of the most common injuries resulting from nursing home negligence.

MALNUTRITION AND DEHYDRATION

Malnutrition and dehydration may occur if the nursing home staff fails to provide adequate food and/or water to the resident. Malnutrition results from the lack of a proper diet, including essential vitamins and nutrients. It can be a serious, life-threatening condition for an elderly person. Dehydration results from inadequate hydration—i.e., the individual's loss of fluids exceeds his or her intake of fluids. Dehydration can also lead to a variety of serious health problems and death. Thus, it is crucial that nursing homes recognize the increased risk of malnutrition and dehydration that elderly people face, and take adequate preventive measures.

Malnutrition may occur in a nursing home setting if the resident is unable to properly eat on their own. Statistics show that almost half of all nursing home residents require some assistance in feeding. Signs of malnutrition may include, but are not limited to weight loss; wasted muscles; swollen lips, gums or tongue; dull eyes; and pale skin.

Dehydration may occur because the resident neglects to consume enough fluids, or due to the effects of medication, such as diuretics or laxatives. Signs of dehydration may include but are not limited to dry skin, dry mouth, sunken eyes, and concentrated urine. Blood tests may also indicate dehydration.

Unfortunately, these conditions often occur because of nursing home negligence. For example, if a nursing home is understaffed, there is not enough manpower or time to make sure all of the residents are properly fed and hydrated. In addition, the lack of training of nursing home staff makes it unlikely that they would be able to recognize the signs of malnutrition or dehydration until the condition has progressed to a dangerous level.

PRESSURE SORES

Pressure Sores, more commonly known as bedsores, are painful skin ulcers that result from prolonged pressure on a body part that has a thin covering of skin over bone, such as the tailbone, shoulders, elbows, etc. In a nursing home setting, bedsores are often caused by the presence of moisture due to wet sheets or clothing, or the failure of the staff to regularly reposition a bedridden patient. Bedsores may also be caused by dehydration and malnutrition.

Bedsores are most prevalent in residents who are over the age of 75; incontinent; underweight; immobile; and/or have serious underlying medical conditions. Bedsores are extremely painful and a serious health problem. If the ulcers become too deep or infected, they can lead to death. Nevertheless, this condition can be cured and prevented with adequate care.

The law requires a nursing home to ensure that a resident does not develop bedsores to the extent the condition is avoidable. If the development of bedsores is avoidable, and is due to the nursing home's lack of care, the nursing home may be liable for negligence. In order to determine whether the condition was preventable, one must consider a number of factors concerning the care given, including: whether an immobile resident was regularly repositioned; whether care was taken to change wet sheets and clothing; the condition of the resident's skin upon admission; the severity of the bedsores; whether a health care professional was called to examine the resident's condition; and whether the resident had any underlying medical problems that contributed to the condition.

If a resident has developed bedsores, and you are dissatisfied with the way the nursing home is treating the condition, the resident should be taken to a hospital emergency room for evaluation and treatment.

FALLS

Many nursing home injuries result from falls. Many of these falls lead to serious injuries, such as fractures, and even death. The law requires a nursing home to take safety precautions to prevent accidental falls, including adequate supervision and devices, such as handrails to assist elderly residents in walking down hallways. When a resident is admitted, his or her risk of falling should be assessed to determine whether the resident needs any special device to prevent a fall, such as a walker.

Although some falls are purely accidental, and noone is to blame, some falls are caused entirely by the negligence of the nursing home. Such falls may be caused by dimly lit passageways; wet floors; cluttered hallways; lack of bedrails; employees who are improperly trained in lifting residents; improper bed heights; etc.

If a nursing home was put on notice that a resident was at risk for falling, and they failed to take preventive measures, or if they created the unsafe condition that caused the fall, the nursing home may be liable for negligence. Depending on the severity of the injury, a lawsuit may be initiated to recover for the resident's damages, including his or her pain and suffering as a result of the fall.

WANDERING AND ELOPEMENT

Wandering is a common problem among nursing home residents who are cognitively impaired. Such persons are found walking around the nursing home aimlessly, without any awareness of their surroundings. This can lead to serious injury. Elopement is a type of wandering, however, it refers to the ability of the resident to leave the facility undetected and unsupervised.

The law requires that a nursing home provide adequate supervision to prevent incidents of wandering and elopement. When a person is admitted to the nursing home, his or her risk of wandering or elopement must be evaluated and included in the resident's plan of care. Residents who are at high risk for wandering and elopement are those who suffer from dementia, Alzheimer's disease, and those who are on medications that may cause confusion.

A nursing home may be liable for negligence if it is aware of a resident's tendency for wandering or elopement, it fails to take adequate security measures to prevent this behavior, and the resident is injured as a result. Inadequate security measures may include, but are not limited to understaffing; failure to properly train employees on wandering and elopement behaviors; the absence of alarm systems designed to prevent wandering and/or elopement; and the failure of employees to properly supervise at risk residents.

CHAPTER 5:
NURSING HOME ABUSE

IN GENERAL

It is a sad and unfortunate fact that many elderly residents of nursing homes have been subjected to criminal acts of abuse. While neglect, as discussed in Chapter 4, involves the failure to provide reasonable care for a person, abuse refers to intentionally causing pain or injury to another.

Nursing home abuse may take many forms, and includes physical abuse, such as assault and battery; sexual assault and battery, including sexual molestation and rape; mental and emotional abuse; verbal abuse and intimidation, the deprivation of food or water for prolonged periods of time; unreasonable and prolonged physical restraints; unreasonable seclusion; and corporal punishment.

Federal and state laws provide that a resident in a nursing home has the right to be free from physical, sexual, and mental abuse, as well as involuntary seclusion. In addition, there are federal and state regulations aimed at preventing the employment of individuals who have been convicted of abuse, neglect or maltreatment in a health care setting.

There are a number of agencies that should be contacted if a nursing home resident is subjected to abuse, including the local law enforcement officials; the state office of aging; the state long-term care ombudsman; the state licensing and certification agency; and the state's adult protective services office.

PHYSICAL ABUSE

Physical abuse is the intentional use of physical force upon an individual that is likely to result in bodily injury or pain. Physical abuse occurs when a staff member or co-resident physically assaults the resident. This may include but is not limited to hitting, punching, shoving, slapping, kicking, burning, shaking, or force-feeding the resident.

In the nursing home setting, physical abuse is extremely serious due to the often fragile condition of the elderly residents. Elderly people are more susceptible to fractures because their bones are generally more brittle. In addition, the thinness and lack of elasticity in their skin causes them to bruise and cut more easily.

Indications that a nursing home resident may be the victim of physical abuse include unexplained black eyes; sprains; fractures; cuts and bruises; internal bleeding; and hair loss. In addition, if a family member is denied access to the resident, this should raise a warning signal that something may be wrong. In such a case, carefully examine the resident and watch for any unusual change in the resident's behavior, such as anxiety, fear or stress, particularly if there is a strong reaction to certain nursing home employees or co-residents.

Be aware that if the resident does not admit being victimized, he or she may fear retaliation from the abusive staff member. It may take some time to convince the victim that they do not have anything to fear. Once the abuse has been confirmed, immediately contact local law enforcement authorities and obtain medical help.

If you suspect that the resident has been the victim of physical abuse, and there is evidence of possible abuse, but he or she will not admit it, or is unable to communicate effectively, law enforcement should still be called and the person should be taken for medical evaluation. If you are not sure whether abuse has occurred, you should still confidentially convey your suspicions to the nursing home administrator, and ask that the situation be monitored.

SEXUAL ABUSE

Sexual abuse generally involves any type of nonconsensual sexual contact, including improper touching and forced sexual acts, such as rape and sodomy. Sadly, elderly nursing home residents fall victim to sexual abuse because of their fragility and inability to defend themselves. In addition, many nursing home residents are unable to effectively communicate, making them easy prey for sexual predators, including staff members and co-residents.

Indications that a nursing home resident may be the victim of sexual abuse include unexplained bruising in the genital area, buttocks or breasts; difficulty walking or sitting; vaginal and/or anal bleeding; genital infections, irritation or injury; sexually transmitted diseases; and torn or bloody undergarments. Again, carefully examine the resident and watch for any unusual change in the resident's behavior, such as anxiety, fear or stress, particularly if there is a strong reaction to certain nursing home employees or co-residents.

As with suspected physical abuse described above, if there are indications of sexual abuse, law enforcement authorities must be notified and the resident must be taken for medical evaluation and treatment, whether or not the resident admits that sexual abuse has taken place.

MENTAL ABUSE

Mental abuse involves the intentional infliction of emotional distress, fear and anguish through the use of verbal and/or nonverbal actions. Under the law, nursing home residents have the right to be treated with dignity and respect, which includes the right to be free from mental and emotional abuse.

Verbal abuse by nursing home employees is a common problem in nursing homes, and may occur when a staff member ridicules, harasses, threatens, curses, berates and/or ignores a resident. Often staff members lack the training and compassion needed to deal with the problems of the elderly, such as the inability to control bodily functions.

Verbal abuse may be directed at an individual resident or generally expressed in front of a group of residents, in order to degrade and demoralize them. Verbal threats are generally directed at a specific resident. For example, the resident may be threatened with physical harm or some type of deprivation if they don't finish their food, or if they soil their clothing.

Residents who are subjected to emotional or verbal abuse are often afraid to speak out, or ask for items of necessity, for fear of being ridiculed. This can lead to serious consequences. For example, a resident may be afraid to bring a physical complaint to the attention of the staff, which could lead to serious illness, or they may fear asking for a glass of water because they do not want to face verbal abuse, which could in turn lead to dehydration.

FINANCIAL ABUSE

Financial abuse occurs when a staff member deliberately steals, misplaces, or misuses a resident's belongings without consent, such as the resident's money, jewelry, clothing or other personal property.

NURSING HOME LIABILITY FOR ABUSE

Under the law, nursing home residents have the right to be free from physical, sexual and emotional abuse. Nursing homes have a duty to thoroughly investigate the background of the employees it hires. In addition, if the investigation reveals that an applicant has criminal convictions that would indicate their unsuitability for working in the nursing home setting, including convictions for crimes such as child abuse or sexual assault, the nursing home has an obligation to report that individual.

When abuse occurs, the nursing home itself may be liable for the conduct of the offending staff member if:

1. The nursing home failed to conduct an adequate background investigation which would have revealed a staff member's propensity for violence or sexual assault.

2. The nursing home was understaffed and failed to employ a sufficient number of employees to supervise the staff and residents.

3. The nursing home failed to properly train its employees concerning physical, sexual and mental abuse.

4. The nursing home failed to properly supervise its employees.

5. The nursing home continued to employ a person who exhibited signs of aggression or improper sexual tendencies towards residents.

THE NATIONAL CENTER FOR ELDER ABUSE

The National Center for Elder Abuse is a federal grant-funded partnership of leading organizations involved with preventing elder abuse. The organization provides comprehensive information about elder abuse, including hotline reporting numbers, elder abuse laws, and other helpful information and resources.

A table of state statutes concerning elder abuse is set forth at Appendix 13.

CHAPTER 6:
REMEDIES

IN GENERAL

If it appears that a nursing home resident is not getting the care they are entitled to, there are many steps a resident and/or family members can take to resolve the problem. The remedy one chooses to pursue depends, in large part, on the severity of the problem. Minor problems may be resolved informally. More serious problems may require government agency intervention or litigation.

It is important to keep a journal which sets forth all of your grievances concerning the quality of care at the nursing home. Take notes of all details, including names, dates, witnesses, conversations, etc. If you are able to take photographs, preferably without the knowledge of the nursing home staff, this will assist in creating a record for future use should it become necessary.

MEETING WITH THE STAFF

The first step in addressing a problem is to have a meeting with the nursing home staff, provided the grievance is relatively minor or concerns an isolated incident. A friendly discussion often helps to keep a minor problem from developing into a more serious situation.

Frequent verbal and physical contact with the nursing home and the resident is the best way to ensure that your loved one is receiving proper care. It is also an important reminder to the staff to know that the resident is being carefully monitored. Nevertheless, there are some nursing homes that are so understaffed, or that employ individuals lacking the proper training and compassion, that complaints must be taken to a higher level, as set forth below.

THE FAMILY COUNCIL

Most nursing homes have a family council where concerned family members meet and express their grievances with the nursing home staff. In

Medicare and Medicaid-approved nursing homes, residents and families have a right to form these councils and meet privately in the nursing home. If there is no existing family council, organize a new council.

If a number of families get together and present their complaints to the nursing home administrator, there is a better chance those concerns will be addressed. In addition, the family council can join with the resident council for even greater strength.

ADVOCACY GROUPS

There are many nursing home advocacy groups throughout the country. These organizations provide information to residents and their family members who have complaints about the care the resident is receiving in a nursing home. These groups often lobby for stronger legislation to protect the rights of nursing home residents. Information about advocacy groups in your area may be obtained by contacting your state's agency on aging or one of the national organizations for the elderly.

A directory of state agencies on aging is set forth at Appendix 6, and a directory of national organizations for the elderly is set forth at Appendix 7 of this almanac.

The Long-Term Care Ombudsman

The Long-Term Care Ombudsman are advocates for nursing home residents who are funded under the Older Americans Act. They are concerned with improving the quality of care in nursing homes nationwide. They offer advice to nursing home residents and their families, and investigate individual complaints of nursing home neglect and abuse.

The Ombudsman are often able to resolve minor problems that occur between the nursing home and the resident. If they are unable to do so, or if the allegations are particularly grievous, they will refer the case to a higher authority, such as the state licensing agency.

A directory of State Offices of Long-Term Care Ombudsman is set forth at Appendix 8.

LEGAL SERVICES FOR THE ELDERLY

There are a number of nonprofit legal services organizations that will provide free legal advice and representation to nursing home residents that concern violations of the resident's rights under the law.

Most nursing homes accept Medicaid and/or Medicare. They are therefore obligated to comply with federal regulations governing nursing homes, including the provisions of the Nursing Home Reform Act, as set forth in

Chapter 3 of this almanac. If a nursing home that accepts federal assistance fails to comply with the law, in addition to other remedies, the residents may bring a claim for medical assistance fraud.

Although these nonprofit legal services organizations do not represent individuals in specific personal injury lawsuits against a nursing home, their involvement in the grievance process may go a long way in resolving the problem. Nursing homes do not want to be under the scrutiny of such an organization and possibly face legal action for violations of the law. Residents who want to pursue individual personal injury actions must hire a private attorney, as set forth below.

A directory of national legal services for the elderly is set forth at Appendix 14.

STATE LICENSING AGENCIES

A complaint can be filed with the state licensing and certification agency. These are government offices, generally organized under the State Department of Health. These government offices are responsible for determining whether a particular nursing home has met both the state licensing requirements and any federal regulations concerning quality of care standards.

The state licensing agencies undertake yearly inspections—also known as surveys—of each nursing home. Violations can be brought to the attention of the agency, which will undertake a complaint investigation. The state is required to investigate all complaints in a timely manner. However, if it is alleged that a dangerous condition exists in the nursing home, which is putting the residents at risk of immediate injury, the agency is required to investigate within two days of receiving the complaint.

You can request that the complaint remain confidential, however, the facility is often able to discover the name of the complainant at some point in the investigation. Making a complaint while the resident is still in the nursing home also raises real concerns about retaliation.

The state can take a range of actions against a nursing home that has violated the law. For example, they can order the nursing home to comply with the law and correct the violations. They can assess a fine or suspend the facility's license to operate. They can also appoint a temporary administrator in the facility to oversee compliance. In serious situations, the state can stop federal Medicare and Medicaid funding to the nursing home. Insofar as most nursing homes rely on the federal Medicare and Medicaid program for most, if not all of their business, this can effectively close down a particularly substandard nursing home.

THE HEALTH CARE FINANCING ADMINISTRATION

The Health Care Financing Administration (HCFA) is the federal program that oversees the state inspection agencies. If the state agency does not resolve the complaint in a timely manner, a complaint may be filed with the HCFA.

The complaint should describe the problem, including dates, names, and witnesses. The length of time the condition has existed should also be stated. The complaint should also state whether the problem is an emergency or is placing the resident in immediate danger of injury. Set forth what steps you have taken to try and resolve the complaint.

LITIGATION

If the resident has suffered a serious injury resulting from the nursing home's neglect or abuse, it may be necessary to bring a private lawsuit against the facility. Although this may be time consuming and expensive, it forces the nursing home to address the problem. The type of lawsuit which must be initiated depends on the type of injury sustained.

Nursing homes have a duty to protect the residents form harm. Negligence occurs when the nursing home, or its employee, fails to meet the proper standard of care required, and this failure results in an injury to the resident. When the nursing home is understaffed, or the employees are not properly trained or supervised, this can lead to neglect and abuse of the residents.

As set forth in Chapters 4 and 5, residents may become dehydrated and malnourished, or develop pressure sores, due to neglect. There may be inadequate safety measures, or the use of improper restraint techniques, which may lead to physical injuries. More serious cases may involve physical, emotional and sexual abuse.

When a lawyer is hired on behalf of the resident, he or she will investigate the complaint, evaluate the injury and make a determination as to who is responsible. Successful litigation may result in a monetary award to compensate the resident for his or her medical expenses, and pain and suffering. In cases of gross negligence, or intentional acts, the resident may be entitled to recover punitive damages as well. Punitive damages are assessed as a way of punishing the wrongful party.

Medical Negligence

If it is determined that the injury was caused by medical negligence—i.e., the carelessness of a health care provider—this is known as medical malpractice. In a nursing home setting, this may occur if the resident is prescribed the wrong medicine, or is either over or under-dosed, and harm results. Medical mistakes may also involve the failure to adequately diagnose and treat a resident.

If the resident is injured due to a medical mistake, he or she may have a cause of action against the medical director and/or attending physicians, the nursing administrator and/or nursing staff, and the nursing home. Medical malpractice cases are subject to more stringent standards than a general negligence action. In addition, most states have shortened statutes of limitation for medical malpractice claims. This means that the claim must be filed in court sooner than other types of personal injury claims, or the injured person will have no recourse. Therefore, if it is suspected that a medical mistake caused the resident's injury, it is important to consult an attorney as soon as possible.

Due to the complexities involving medical malpractice litigation, a detailed discussion of medical malpractice law is not possible in this almanac. More detailed information on medical malpractice may be found in this author's legal almanac entitled The Law of Medical Malpractice, also published by Oceana Publications.

APPENDIX 1:
NUMBER OF NURSING HOME RESIDENTS AGE 65 OR OLDER, BY AGE GROUP (1985-1995-1997-1999) (IN THOUSANDS)

AGE GROUP	1985	1995	1997	1999
65 OR OLDER	1,318	1,423	1,465	1,469
65 TO 74	212	190	198	195
75 TO 84	509	512	528	518
85 OR OLDER	597	720	738	757

Source: National Nursing Home Survey.

APPENDIX 2:
NUMBER OF MALE NURSING HOME RESIDENTS AGE 65 OR OLDER (1985-1995-1997-1999) (IN THOUSANDS)

AGE GROUP	1985	1995	1997	1999
65 OR OLDER	334	357	372	378
65 TO 74	81	79	81	84
75 TO 84	141	144	159	150
85 OR OLDER	113	133	132	144

Source: National Nursing Home Survey.

APPENDIX 3:
NUMBER OF FEMALE NURSING HOME RESIDENTS AGE 65 OR OLDER (1985-1995-1997-1999) (IN THOUSANDS)

AGE GROUP	1985	1995	1997	1999
65 OR OLDER	984	1,066	1,093	1,092
65 TO 74	132	111	118	111
75 TO 84	368	368	369	368
85 OR OLDER	485	587	606	613

Source: National Nursing Home Survey.

APPENDIX 4:
MEDICARE PATIENTS' STATEMENT OF RIGHTS

As a Medicare beneficiary, you have certain guaranteed rights. These rights protect you when you get health care; they assure you access to needed health care services; and they protect you against unethical practices. You have these Medicare rights whether you are in the Original Medicare Plan or another Medicare health plan. Your rights include:

1. The right to protection from discrimination in marketing and enrollment practices.

2. The right to information about what is covered and how much you have to pay.

3. The right to information about all treatment options available to you. You have the right to information about all your health care treatment options from your health care provider. Medicare forbids its health plans from making any rules that would stop a doctor from telling you everything you need to know about your health care, including treatment options. If you think your Medicare health plan may have kept your health care provider from telling you everything you need to know about your health care treatment options, you have a right to appeal.

4. The right to receive emergency care. If you have severe pain, an injury, sudden illness, or a suddenly worsening illness that you believe may cause your health serious danger without immediate care, you have the right to receive emergency care. You never need prior approval for emergency care, and you may receive emergency care anywhere in the United States.

5. The right to appeal decisions to deny or limit payment for medical care. If you are in the Original Medicare Plan, you have the right to appeal a denial of payment for a service you have been provided. Likewise, if you are enrolled in one of the other Medicare health plans, you have the right to appeal the plan's denial for a service to be provided.

As a Medicare beneficiary, you always have the right to appeal these decisions.

6. The right to know how your Medicare health plan pays its doctors. If you request information on how a Medicare health plan pays its doctors, the plan must give it to you in writing. You also have the right to know whether your doctor has a financial interest in a health care facility, such as a laboratory, since it could affect the medical advice he or she gives you.

7. The right to choose a women's health specialist.

8. The right, if you have a complex or serious medical condition, to receive a treatment plan that includes direct access to a specialist.

If you believe that any of your rights have been violated, please call the State Health Insurance Assistance Program in your State.

Source: Social Security Administration.

APPENDIX 5:
NURSING HOME NEEDS ASSESSMENT SURVEY

WHY DO YOU NEED A NURSING HOME?

[ ] Individual can no longer care for him/herself

[ ] Individual requires more care than can be provided by our family

[ ] Individual has extensive medical needs

[ ] Physician recommendation

[ ] Discharged from hospital and requires temporary skilled care before returning home

INDIVIDUAL CURRENTLY HAS THE FOLLOWING NEEDS (CHECK AS MANY AS APPLY)

Nursing Care Level Requirements

[ ] Supervision only

[ ] Assistance with daily living activities

[ ] Therapy

[ ] 24-hour nursing

[ ] Intensive nursing

[ ] Other

Medical Conditions

[ ] Alzheimer's disease

[ ] Cancer

[ ] Cardiovascular disease

[ ] Chronic pain

[ ] Dementia

[ ] Developmentally disabled

[ ] Head trauma

[ ] Hematologic condition

[ ] Mental disease

[ ] Neurological disease

[ ] Neuromuscular disease

[ ] Orthopedic/skeletal problems

[ ] Pulmonary disease

[ ] Para/quadriplegic

[ ] Stroke

[ ] Trauma

[ ] Wound

[ ] Other

Therapies Recommended By Physician

[ ] Physical therapy

[ ] Occupational therapy

[ ] Speech therapy

[ ] Respiratory therapy

[ ] Reality therapy

[ ] Other

Equipment and Supplies

[ ] Wheel chair

[ ] Prosthetics

[ ] Ventilator

[ ] Special bed

[ ] Intravenous drugs

[ ] Prescription drugs

[ ] Medical supplies

[ ] Oxygen

[ ] Other

Other Medical Specialists Needed on a Regular Basis

[ ] Dentist

[ ] Dietician

[ ] Opthamologist

[ ] Physician

[ ] Podiatrist

[ ] Other

Individual Requires Help With The Following Activities of Daily Living

[ ] Personal care

[ ] Bathing

[ ] Continence

[ ] Dressing

[ ] Eating

[ ] Mobility

[ ] Toileting

[ ] Using the telephone

[ ] Shopping

[ ] Preparing meals

[ ] Housekeeping

[ ] Laundry

[ ] Transportation

[ ] Taking medications

[ ] Handling finances

[ ] Other

Cultural and Social Needs (Special Needs)

[ ] Language (if not English)

[ ] Culturally-based special diet

[ ] Medically prescribed special diet

[ ] Other

Religion

[ ] Religious affiliation

Social activities preferred

[ ] Cards and games

[ ] Movies

[ ] Prayer groups

[ ] Arts and crafts

[ ] Television

[ ] Reading

[ ] Pet therapy

[ ] Social events

[ ] Outdoor activities

[ ] Interaction with others

[ ] Other

FACILITY PREFERENCES

[ ] Private room

[ ] Semi-private room

[ ] Small facility (Less than 100 beds)

[ ] Medium facility (101 to 300 beds)

[ ] Large facility (over 300 beds)

FAMILY NEEDS

[ ] Family is current care provider

[ ] Is home-based care an option?

[ ] Is respite care (part-time nursing home care) an alternative?

[ ] Is adult day care an option?

[ ] Family lives in town

[ ] Family lives out of town

LOCATION

[ ] City preferred

[ ] County preferred

[ ] State preferred

[ ] Location near family and friends?

[ ] Location near a hospital?

[ ] Location near a doctor's office or clinic?

FINANCIAL—HOW WILL YOU PAY FOR CARE?

[ ] Private pay

[ ] Medicare

[ ] Medicaid

[ ] Veteran's benefits

[ ] Private long-term care insurance

[ ] HMO or managed care

[ ] Other

TRANSPORTATION

[ ] Who will transport the individual to off-site appointments if necessary?

    [ ] Family will provide

    [ ] Facility must provide

LEGAL

Does the individual have a will? Yes/No

Is a durable power of attorney in place? Yes/No

Any life support directives? Yes/No

Does the individual have a living will? Yes/No

Source: Nursing Home INFO.

APPENDIX 6:
DIRECTORY OF STATE AGENCIES ON AGING

STATE	REGION	AGENCY	ADDRESS	TELEPHONE/ FAX	E-MAIL
Alabama	Region IV	Alabama Department of Senior Services	770 Washington Avenue Montgomery, AL 36130-1851	(334) 242-5743 (334) 242-5594	N/A
Alaska	Region X	Alaska Commission on Aging	P.O. Box 110209 Juneau, AK 99811-0209	(907) 465-3250 (907) 465-4716	acoa@admin.state.ak.us
Arizona	Region IX	Aging and Adult Administration	1789 West Jefferson Street Phoenix, AZ 85007	(602) 542-4446 (602) 542-6575	N/A
Arkansas	Region VI	Division Aging and Adult Services	1417 Donaghey Plaza South Little Rock, AR 72203-1437	(501) 682-2441 (501) 682-8155	ron.tatus@mail.state.ar.us
California	Region IX	California Department of Aging	1600 K Street Sacramento, CA 95814	(916) 322-5290 (916) 324-1903	lterry@aging.state.ca.us

STATE	REGION	AGENCY	ADDRESS	TELEPHONE/FAX	E-MAIL
Colorado	Region VIII	Aging and Adult Services	1575 Sherman Street Denver, CO 80203	(303) 866-2800 (303) 866-2696	viola.mcneace@state.co.us
Connecticut	Region I	Division of Elderly Services	25 Sigourney Street Hartford, CT 06106-5033	(860) 424-5298 (860) 424-4966	adultserv.dss@po.state.ct.us
Delaware	Region III	Delaware Division of Services for Aging	1901 North DuPont Highway New Castle, DE 19720	(302) 577-4791 (302) 577-4793	dsaapdinfo@state.de.us
Florida	Region IV	Department of Elder Affairs	4040 Esplanade Way Tallahassee, FL 32399-7000	(850) 414-2000 (850) 414-2004	information@elderaffairs.org
Georgia	Region IV	Division of Aging Services	2 Peachtree Street N.E. Atlanta, GA 30303-3142	(404) 657-5258 (404) 657-5285	dhrconstituentservices@dhr.state.ga.us
Hawaii	Region IX	Hawaii Executive Office on Aging	250 South Hotel Street Honolulu, HI 96813-2831	(808) 586-0100 (808) 586-0185	eoa@mail.health.state.hi.us
Idaho	Region X	Idaho Commission on Aging	P.O. Box 83720 Boise, ID 83720-0007	(208) 334-3833 (208) 334-3033	N/A
Illinois	Region V	Illinois Department on Aging	421 East Capitol Avenue Springfield, IL 62701-1789	(217) 785-3356 (217) 785-4477	ilsenior@aging.state.il.us
Indiana	Region V	Bureau of Aging and In-Home Services	402 W. Washington Street P.O. Box 7083 Indianapolis, IN 46207-7083	(317) 232-7020 (317) 232-7867	jlmiller@fssa.state.in.us
Iowa	Region VII	Iowa Department of Elder Affairs	200 Tenth Street Des Moines, IA 50309-3609	(515) 242-3333 (515) 242-3300	sherry.james@dea.state.ia.us
Kansas	Region VII	Department on Aging	503 S. Kansas Ave. Topeka, KS 66603-3404	(785) 296-4986 (785) 296-0256	wwwmail@aging.state.ks.us

STATE	REGION	AGENCY	ADDRESS	TELEPHONE/ FAX	E-MAIL
Kentucky	Region IV	Office of Aging Services	275 East Main Street Frankfort, KY 40621	(502) 564-6930 (502) 564-4595	N/A
Louisiana	Region VI	Governor's Office of Elderly Affairs	P.O. Box 80374 Baton Rouge, LA 70898-0374	(225) 342-7100 (225) 342-7133	PFARceneaux@goea.state. la.us
Maine	Region I	Bureau of Elder and Adult Services	35 Anthony Avenue Augusta, ME 04333	(207) 624-5335 (207) 624-5361	webmaster_beas@state.me.us
Maryland	Region III	Maryland Department of Aging	301 West Preston Street Baltimore, MD 21201-2374	(410) 767-1100 (410) 333-7943	ptc@mail.ooa.state.md.us
Massachusetts	Region I	Massachusetts Executive Office of Elder Affairs	One Ashburton Place Boston, MA 02108	(617) 727-7750 (617) 727-9368	www.state.ma.us/elder
Michigan	Region V	Michigan Office of Services to the Aging	611 W. Ottawa, N. Ottawa Tower P.O. Box 30676 Lansing, MI 48909	(517) 373-8230 (517) 373-4092	N/A
Minnesota	Region V	Minnesota Board on Aging	444 Lafayette Road St. Paul, MN 55155-3843	(651) 296-2770 (651) 297-7855	N/A
Missouri	Region VII	Division of Senior Services	615 Howerton Court Jefferson City, MO 65102-1337	(573) 751-3082 (573) 751-8687	pwoodsma@mail.state.mo.us
Montana	Region VIII	Senior and Long Term Care Division	P.O. Box 4210 Helena, MT 59620	(406) 444-4077 (406) 444-7743	N/A
Nebraska	Region VII	Division on Aging	1343 M Street Lincoln, NE 68509-5044	(402) 471-2307 (402) 471-4619	mark.intermill@hhss.state.ne. us
Nevada	Region IX	Nevada Division for Aging Services	3416 Goni Road Carson City, NV 89706	(775) 687-4210 (775) 687-4264	dascc@govmail.state.nv.us

STATE	REGION	AGENCY	ADDRESS	TELEPHONE/ FAX	E-MAIL
New Hampshire	Region I	Division of Elderly and Adult Services	129 Pleasant Street Concord, NH 03301	(603) 271-4680, (603) 271-4643	N/A
New Jersey	Region II	New Jersey Division of Senior Affairs	P.O Box 807 Trenton, NJ 08625-0807	(609) 943-3436, (609) 588-3317	seniors@doh.state.nj.us
New Mexico	Region VI		228 East Palace Avenue Santa Fe, NM 87501	(505) 827-7640, (505) 827-7649	nmaoa@state.nm.us
New York	Region II	New York State Office for The Aging	2 Empire State Plaza Albany, NY 12223-1251	(518) 474-5731, (518) 474-0608	nysofa@ofa.state.ny.us
North Carolina	Region IV	Division of Aging	2101 Mail Service Center Raleigh, NC 27699-2101	(919) 733-3983, (919) 733-0443	mary.beth@ncmail.net
North Dakota	Region VIII	Aging Services Division	600 South 2nd Street Bismarck, ND 58504	(701) 328-891, (800) 451-8693, (701) 328-8989	dhssrinf@state.nd.us
Ohio	Region V	Ohio Department of Aging	50 West Broad Street Columbus, OH 43215-5928	(614) 466-5500, (614) 466-5741	N/A
Oklahoma	Region VI	Aging Services Division	312 N.E. 28th Street Oklahoma City, OK 73125	(405) 521-2281, (405) 521-2086	Cynthia.Kinkade@okdhs.org
Oregon	Region X	Seniors and People with Disabilities	500 Summer Street N.E., Salem, OR 97301-1073	(503) 945-5811, (503) 373-7823	sdsd.info@state.or.us
Pennsylvania	Region III	Pennsylvania Department of Aging	555 Walnut Street Harrisburg, PA 17101-1919	(717) 783-1550, (717) 772-3382	aging@state.pa.us
Rhode Island	Region I	Department of Elderly Affairs	160 Pine Street Providence, RI 02903-3708	(401) 222-2858, (401) 222-2130	larry@dea.state.ri.us

Nursing Home Negligence

STATE	REGION	AGENCY	ADDRESS	TELEPHONE/ FAX	E-MAIL
South Carolina	Region IV	Office of Senior and Long Term Care Services	P.O. Box 8206 Columbia, SC 29202-8206	(803) 898-2501, (803) 898-4515	N/A
South Dakota	Region VIII	Office of Adult Services and Aging	700 Governors Drive Pierre, SD 57501-2291	(605) 773-3656, (605) 773-6834	asaging@dss.state.sd.us
Tennessee	Region IV	Commission on Aging and Disability	500 Deaderick Street Nashville, Tennessee 37243-0860	(615) 741-2056, (615) 741-3309	N/A
Texas	Region VI	Texas Department on Aging	4900 North Lamar Austin, TX 78751-2316	(512) 424-6840, (512) 424-6890	mail@tdoa.state.tx.us
Utah	Region VIII	Division of Aging & Adult Services	120 North 200 West Salt Lake City, UT 84145-0500	(801) 538-3910, (801) 538-4395	DAAS@hs.state.ut.us
Vermont	Region I	Vermont Department of Aging and Disabilities	103 South Main Street, Waterbury, VT 05671-2301	(802) 241-2400, (802) 241-2325	patrick@dad.state.vt.us
Virginia	Region III	Virginia Department for the Aging	1600 Forest Avenue Richmond, VA 23229	(804) 662-9333, (804) 662-9354	aging@vdh.state.va.us

APPENDIX 7:
DIRECTORY OF NATIONAL ORGANIZATIONS FOR THE ELDERLY

AGENCY	WEBSITE	FUNCTION
Administration on Aging	http://www.aoa.gov	Federal government agency that provides information to older persons and their families on age-related issues
Alzheimer's Association	http://www.alz.org	Provides information for families looking for residential care for someone with Alzheimer's disease
American Association of Homes and Services for the Aging	http://www.aahsa.org/public/consumer.htm	National organization consisting of more than 5,000 not-for-profit nursing homes, continuing care retirement communities, senior housing and assisted living facilities, and community services for the elderly

AGENCY	WEBSITE	FUNCTION
American Association of Retired Persons	http://www.aarp.org	A non-profit, non-partisan association dedicated to shaping and enriching the American aging experience
American Geriatrics Society	http://www.americangeriatrics.org	A professional organization of health-care providers dedicated to improving the health and well-being of older people and effecting change in the provision of health care to older Americans
Association for the Protection of the Elderly	http://www.apeape.org	An association dedicated to improving nursing home conditions and educating nursing home residents and their families on quality of care issues
The Centers for Medicare and Medicaid Services	http://www.medicare.gov/nhcompare/home.asp	Federal agency that oversees Medicare and Medicaid and has a web site to help people in their search for a nursing home
Elder Abuse Prevention Information & Resource Guide	http://www.oaktrees.org/elder	Organization dedicated to stopping the abuse of the elderly
Eldercare Locator	http://www.aoa.dhhs.gov/elderpage/locator.html	Nationwide directory assistance service designed to help older persons and caregivers locate local support resources for aging Americans
The National Center for Elder Abuse	http://www.elderabusecenter.org	Federal grant-funded partnership of leading organizations involved with preventing elder abuse

AGENCY	WEBSITE	FUNCTION
National Citizens' Coalition for Nursing Home Reform	http://www.nccnhr.org	Provides information on choosing a nursing home and other information for families who want quality nursing home care
National Health Law Program	http://www.healthlaw.org	A national public interest law firm seeking to improve health care for America's elderly, poor, disabled, and minority citizens
National Institute on Aging	http://www.nia.nih.gov	Federal agency of the National Institutes of Health that promotes healthy aging by supporting and conducting research and public education on aging issues
National Senior Citizen Law Center	http://www.nsclc.org	National advocates devoted to promoting the independence and well-being of elderly and disabled people
Nursing Home Info	http://www.nursinghomeinfo.com	Financial and Internet marketing consulting firm specializing in the senior care area which provides nationwide nursing home information
United States Department of Health and Human Services	http://aspe.os.dhhs.gov	Website devoted to Medicare issues

APPENDIX 8:
DIRECTORY OF STATE OFFICES OF
LONG-TERM CARE OMBUDSMAN

STATE	NAME	ADDRESS	TELEPHONE NUMBER
Alabama	Commission on Aging	770 Washington Avenue, Montgomery, AL 36104	334-242-5743
Alaska	Office of the Older Alaskans Ombudsman	550 W. 7th Avenue, Anchorage, AK 99501	907-334-4480
Arizona	Aging and Adult Administration	1789 West Jefferson Street, Phoenix, AZ 85007	602-542-6454
Arkansas	Arkansas State Office on Aging	P.O. Box 1437, Little Rock, AR 72201	501-682-8952
California	Department of Aging	1600 K Street, Sacramento, CA 95814	916-322-6681
Colorado	Aging and Adult Services Division	455 Sherman Street, Denver, CO 80203	800-288-1376
Connecticut	Department on Aging	25 Sigourney Street, Hartford, CT 06106	860-424-5200
Delaware	Division of Aging	1901 N. Dupont Highway, New Castle, DE 19963	302-255-9390
District of Columbia	Office on Aging	441 4th Street N.W., Washington, DC 20001	202-754-5622
Florida	Program Office of Aging and Adult Services	4040 Esplanade Way, Tallahassee, FL 32399	888-831-0404
Georgia	Office of Aging	2 Peachtree Street N.W., Atlanta, GA 30309	888-454-5826
Hawaii	Executive Office on Aging	250 South Hotel Street, Honolulu, HI 96813	808-586-0100

STATE	NAME	ADDRESS	TELEPHONE NUMBER
Idaho	Office on Aging	State House, Room 114, Boise, ID 83720	208-334-3833
Illinois	Department on Aging	421 East Capitol Avenue Box 7083, Springfield, IL 62706	217-785-3140
Indiana	Department on Aging & Community Services	P.O Box 7083, Indianapolis, IN 46207	800-545-7763
Iowa	Commission on Aging	200 10th Street, Des Moines, IA 50309	515-242-3333
Kansas	Department of Aging	900 S.W. Jackson St., Topeka, KS 66612	785-296-3017
Kentucky	Division for Aging Services	275 East Main Street, 6th Floor, Frankfort, KY 40601	502-564-6930
Louisiana	Office of Elderly Affairs	P.O Box 80374, Baton Rouge, LA 70802	225-342-6872
Maine	Commission on Aging	State House, Station No. 127, Augusta, ME 04333	207-621-1079
Maryland	Office on Aging	301 West Preston Street, Baltimore, MD 21201	410-767-1100
Massachusetts	Department of Elder Affairs	1 Ashburton Place, Boston, MA 02108	617-727-7750
Michigan	Citizens for Better Care	221 N. Pine Street, Lansing, MI 48933	866-485-9393
Minnesota	Office of Ombudsman for Older Minnesotans	444 Lafayette Road, St. Paul, MN 55155	651-296-2770
Mississippi	Mississippi Council on Aging	750 North State Street, Jackson, MS 39202	601-359-4927
Missouri	Division on Aging	P.O. Box 570, Jefferson City, MO 65102	800-309-3282

STATE	NAME	ADDRESS	TELEPHONE NUMBER
Montana	Seniors' Office of Legal and Ombudsman Services,	P.O. Box 4210, Capitol Station, Helena, MT 59604	800-551-3191
Nebraska	Department on Aging	P.O. Box 95044, Lincoln, NE 68509	402-471-2307
Nevada	Division of Aging Services	445 Apple Street, Reno, NV 89502	775-688-2964
New Hampshire	Division of Elderly and Adult Services	129 Pleasant Street, Concord, NH 03301	603-271-4704
New Jersey	Office of the Ombudsman for the Institutionalized Elderly	P.O. Box 807, Trenton, NJ 08625	609-943-4026
New Mexico	State Agency on Aging	1410 San Pedro, Santa Fe, NM 87110	505-827-7640
New York	Office for the Aging	Empire State Plaza, Agency Building No. 2, Albany, NY 12223	518-474-0108
North Carolina	Division of Aging	2101 Mail Service Center, Raleigh, NC 27699	919-733-8395
North Dakota	Aging Services Division	600 S. 2Nd Street, Bismarck, ND 58504	800-451-8693
Ohio	Department of Aging	50 West Broad Street, 9th Floor, Columbus, OH 43215	614-466-1221
Oklahoma	Special Unit on Aging	312 N.E. 28th Street, Oklahoma City, OK 73105	405-521-6734
Oregon	Office of Long-Term Care Ombudsman	3855 Wolverine Drive N.E., Salem, OR 97305	503-378-6533
Pennsylvania	Department of Aging	P.O. Box 1089, Harrisburg, PA 17120	717-783-7247
Rhode Island	Department of Elderly Affairs	422 Post Road, Warwick, RI 02888	401-785-3340

STATE	NAME	ADDRESS	TELEPHONE NUMBER
South Carolina	Division of Ombudsman and Citizens' Service	P.O. Box 8206, Columbia, SC 29202	803-898-2850
South Dakota	Office of Adult Services and Aging	700 Governors Drive, Pierre, SD 57501	605-773-3656
Tennessee	Commission on Aging	706 Church Street, Suite 201, Nashville, TN 37243	615-741-2056
Texas	Department on Aging	P.O. Box 12786, Capitol Station, Austin, TX 78741	512-444-2727
Utah	Division of Aging and Adult Services	120 North 200 West, Salt Lake City, UT 84103	801-538-3924
Vermont	Office on Aging	103 South Main Street, Waterbury, VT 05676	802-241-2400
Virginia	State Long-Term Care Ombudsman	530 East Main Street, Richmond, VA 23219	804-565-1600
Washington	State Long-Term Care Ombudsman	1200 S. 336 Street, Federal Way, Olympia, WA 98093	800-422-1384
West Virginia	Commission on Aging	State Capitol, Charleston, WV 25305	304-558-3317
Wisconsin	Board on Aging and Long Term Care	1402 Pankratz Street, Madison, WI 53704	800-815-0015
Wyoming	State Long-Term Care Ombudsman	P.O. Box 94, Wheatland, WY 82201	307-322-5553

APPENDIX 9:
DIRECTORY OF STATE LICENSING AGENCIES FOR NURSING HOMES

STATE	NAME	DEPARTMENT	ADDRESS	TELEPHONE	FACSIMILE
Alabama	Department of Public Health	Div. Health Care Facilities	P.O. Box 303017, Montgomery, AL 36130-3017	(334) 206-5077	(334) 206-5088
Alaska	Health Facilities	Licensing & Certification	4730 Business Park Boulevard, Suite 18, Bldg. H, Anchorage, AK 99503-7137	(907) 561-8081	(907) 561-3011
Arizona	Department of Health Services	Assurance and Licensure	1647 East Morten Avenue, Suite 220, Phoenix, AZ 85020	(602) 674-4200	(602) 861-0645
Arkansas	Department of Health	Health Facilities Services,	5800 W. 10th Street, Suite 400, Little Rock, AR 72204	(501) 661-2201	(501) 661-2165
California	Department of Health Services	Licensing & Certification	1800 3rd St., Suite 210, P.O. Box 942732, Sacramento, CA 94234-7320	(916) 445-3054	(916) 445-6979
Colorado	Department of Health & Environment	Health Facilities Division	4300 Cherry Creek Drive South, Denver, CO 80222-1530	(303) 692-2800	(303) 691-7822

STATE	NAME	DEPARTMENT	ADDRESS	TELEPHONE	FACSIMILE
Connecticut	Department of Public Health	Division of Health Systems Regulation	410 Capitol Avenue, Hartford, CT 06134-0308	(860) 509-7400	(860) 509-7543
Delaware	Division of Long-Term Care Residents Protection	Health and Social Services	3 Mill Road, Suite 308, Wilmington, DE 19806	(302) 577-6661	(302) 577-6672
District of Columbia	Health Regulation Administration	Division of Licensing and Certification	825 North Capitol Street NE, Washington, DC 20002	(202) 442-5888	(202) 442-9430
Florida	Agency For Health Care Administration	Division for Health Quality Assurance	2727 Mahan Drive, Tallahassee, FL 32308-5403	(850) 487-2528	(850) 487-6240
Georgia	Department of Human Resources	Office of Regulatory Services,	2 Peachtree Street NW, Atlanta, GA 30303-3167	(404) 657-5700	(404) 657-5708
Hawaii	Department of Health	Office of Health Care Assurance	601 Kamokila Blvd., Kapolei, HI 96707	(808) 692-7420	(808) 692-7447
Idaho	Dept. of Health & Welfare	Facility Standards Bureau	P.O. Box 83720, Boise, ID 83720-0036	(208) 334-6626	(208) 364-1888
Illinois	Department of Public Health	Office Health Care Regulation	525 West Jefferson, Springfield, IL 62761	(217) 782-2913	(217) 524-6292
Indiana	State Department of Health	Consumer Health Services Commission	2 North Meridian Street, Indianapolis, IN 46204	(317) 233-7022	(317) 233-7053
Iowa	Department of Inspection & Appeals	Health Facilities Division	Lucas State Office Building, Des Moines, IA 50319-0083	(515) 281-4233	(515) 242-5022
Kansas	Department Health & Environment	Division of Health	1000 SW Jackson, Topeka, KS 66612-1365	(785) 296-1240	(785) 296-1266
Kentucky	Cabinet for Health Services	Division of Long Term Care	275 East Main Street, Frankfort, KY 40621-0001	(502) 564-2800	(502) 562-4268

STATE	NAME	DEPARTMENT	ADDRESS	TELEPHONE	FACSIMILE
Louisiana	Department of Health & Hospitals	Health Standards Section	P.O. Box 3767, Baton Rouge, LA 70821-3767	(225) 342-0415	(225) 342-5292
Maine	Department of Human Services	Division of Licensing and Certification	35 Anthony Avenue, Augusta, ME 04333-0011	(207) 287-9300	(207) 287-9304
Maryland	Department of Health and Mental Hygiene	Office of Health Care Quality	55 Wade Avenue, Baltimore, MD 21228	(410) 402-8001	(410) 402-8215
Massachusetts	Department of Public Health	Division Health Care Quality	10 West Street, Boston, MA 02111	(617) 753-8100	(617) 753-8125
Michigan	Department of Consumer & Industry Svc.	Division of Nursing Home Monitoring	PO Box 30664, Lansing, MI 48909	(517) 241-2506	(517) 241-3354
Minnesota	Department of Health	Division of Facility & Provider Compliance	P.O. Box 64900, St. Paul, MN 55164-0900	(651) 215-8715	(651) 215-8710
Mississippi	Department of Health	Licensure and Certification Division	P.O. Box 1700, Jackson, MS 39215	(601) 576-7300	(601) 354-7230
Missouri	Department of Health and Senior Services	Section for LTC Regulations	PO Box 570, Jefferson City, MO 65102-1337	(573) 526-0721	(573) 751-8493
Montana	Dept. of Health & Human Services	Division of Licensing and Certification	P.O. Box 202953, Helena, MT 59620-2953	(406) 444-2099	(406) 444-3456
Nebraska	Department of Health & Human Services	Health Facility Licensure and Inspection	P.O. Box 95007, Lincoln, NE 68509-5007	(402) 471-0179	(402) 471-0555
Nevada	Department of Human Resources	Bureau of Licensure & Certification	1550 East College Parkway, Carson City, NV 89710	(775) 687-4475	(775) 687-6588
New Hampshire	Bureau of Health Facilities Administration	Department of Health & Human Services	129 Pleasant Street, Concord, NH 03301	(603) 271-4966	(603) 271-5590

STATE	NAME	DEPARTMENT	ADDRESS	TELEPHONE	FACSIMILE
New Jersey	State Department of Health & Senior Services		P.O. Box 367, Trenton, NJ 08625-0367	(609) 633-8980	(609) 633-9060
New Mexico	Department of Health	Licensing & Certification	2040 S. Pachecho, Sante Fe, NM 87505	(505) 476-9025	(505) 476-9026
New York	State Department of Health	Bureau of LTC Services	443 River Street, Troy, NY 12180	(518) 402-1045	(518) 402-1042
North Carolina	Department of Human Services	Licensing and Certification	P.O. Box 29550, Raleigh, NC 27699-2711	(919) 733-7461	(919) 733-8274
North Dakota	State Department of Health	Health Resources Section	600 East Boulevard Avenue, Bismarck, ND 58505-2352	(701) 328-2352	(701) 328-1890
Ohio	Department of Health	Division Quality Assurance	246 North High Street, Columbus, OH 43266-0118	(614) 466-7857	(614) 644-0208
Oklahoma	Department of Health	Protective Health Services	1000 NE 10th Street, Oklahoma City, OK 73117-1299	(405) 271-6868	(405) 271-3442
Oregon	Department of Human Services	Nursing Facility Program Unit	500 Summer St. NE, Salem, OR 97310-1015	(503) 945-6456	(503) 373-7902
Pennsylvania	Department of Health	Division of Nursing Care Facilities,	Health & Welfare Building, Harrisburg, PA 17108	(717) 787-1816	(717) 772-2163
Rhode Island	Department of Health	Facilities Regulation	3 Capitol Hill, Providence, RI 02908-5097	(401) 222-2566	(401) 222-3999
South Carolina	Department of Health & Environmental Control	Bureau of Certification	2600 Bull Street, Columbia, SC 29201-1708	(803) 545-4205	(803) 545-4292
South Dakota	Department of Health	Office of Health Care Facilities	615 East 4th Street, Pierre, SD 57501-5070	(605) 773-3356	(605) 773-6667

STATE	NAME	DEPARTMENT	ADDRESS	TELEPHONE	FACSIMILE
Tennessee	Department of Health	Division of Health Care Facilities	426 5th Avenue, Nashville, TN 37247-0508	(615) 741-7221	(615) 741-7051
Texas	Department of Human Services	Long Term Care Regulatory	PO Box 149030, Austin, TX 78751	(512) 438-2625	(512) 438-2726
Utah	Division of Occupational & Professional Licensing		PO Box 146741, Salt Lake City, UT 84114-6741	(801) 530-6767	(801) 530-6511
Vermont	Department of Aging & Disabilities	Licensing & Protection	103 South Main Street, Waterbury, VT 05671-2306	(802) 241-2345	(802) 241-2358
Virginia	Department of Health	Center for Quality Health Care	3600 West Broad Street, Richmond, VA 23230	(804) 367-2102	(804) 367-2149
Washington	Washington Dept. of Social & Health Services	Residential Care Services	P.O. Box 45600, Olympia, WA 98504-5600	(360) 725-2400	(360) 438-7903
West Virginia	Department of Health	Health Facility Licensure	350 Capitol Street, Charleston, WV 25301-3718	(304) 558-0050	(304) 558-2515
Wisconsin	Department of Health and Family Services	Bureau of Quality Assurance	P.O. Box 2969, Madison, WI 53701-2969	(608) 267-7185	(608) 267-0352
Wyoming	Department of Health	Health Facilities Program	First Bank Building, Cheyenne, WY 82002-0480	(307) 777-7121	(307) 777-5970

APPENDIX 10:
NURSING HOME CHECKLIST

4   ## Nursing Home Checklist

Name of Nursing Home:_____ **Date of Visit:**_____

	Yes	No	Comments
Basic Information			
The nursing home is Medicare-certified.			
The nursing home is Medicaid-certified.			
The nursing home has the level of care needed (e.g. skilled, custodial), and a bed is available.			
The nursing home has special services if needed in a separate unit (e.g. dementia, ventilator, or rehabilitation), and a bed is available.			
The nursing home is located close enough for friends and family to visit.			
Resident Appearance			
Residents are clean, appropriately dressed for the season or time of day, and well groomed.			
Nursing Home Living Spaces			
The nursing home is free from overwhelming unpleasant odors.			
The nursing home appears clean and well-kept.			
The temperature in the nursing home is comfortable for residents.			
The nursing home has good lighting.			
Noise levels in the dining room and other common areas are comfortable.			
Smoking is not allowed or may be restricted to certain areas of the nursing home.			
Furnishings are sturdy, yet comfortable and attractive.			

Nursing Home Checklist

	Yes	No	Comments
Staff			
The relationship between the staff and the residents appears to be warm, polite, and respectful.			
All staff wear name tags.			
Staff knock on the door before entering a resident's room and refer to residents by name.			
The nursing home offers a training and continuing education program for all staff.			
The nursing home does background checks on all staff.			
The guide on your tour knows the residents by name and is recognized by them.			
There is a full-time Registered Nurse (RN) in the nursing home at in the nursing home at all times, other than the Administrator or Director of Nursing.			
The same team of nurses and Certified Nursing Assistants (CNAs) work with the same resident 4 to 5 days per week.			
CNAs work with a reasonable number of residents.			
CNAs are involved in care planning meetings.			
There is a full-time social worker on staff.			
There is a licensed doctor on staff. Is he or she there daily? Can he or she be reached at all times?			
The nursing home's management team has worked together for at least one year.			

Nursing Home Negligence

Nursing Home Checklist

	Yes	No	Comments
Residents' Rooms			
Residents may have personal belongings and/or furniture in their rooms.			
Each resident has storage space (closet and drawers) in his or her room.			
Each resident has a window in his or her bedroom.			
Residents have access to a personal telephone and television.			
Residents have a choice of roommates.			
Water pitchers can be reached by residents.			
There are policies and procedures to protect resident's possessions.			
Hallways, Stairs, Lounges, and Bathrooms			
Exits are clearly marked.			
There are quiet areas where residents can visit with friends and family.			
The nursing home has smoke detectors and sprinklers.			
All common areas, resident rooms, and doorways are designed for wheelchair use.			
There are handrails in the hallways and grab bars in the bathrooms.			
Menus and Food			
Residents have a choice of food items at each meal. (Ask if your favorite foods are served.)			
Nutritious snacks are available upon request.			
Staff help residents eat and drink at mealtimes if help is needed.			

Nursing Home Checklist

4

	Yes	No	Comments
Activities			
Residents, including those who are unable to leave their rooms, may choose to take part in a variety of activities.			
The nursing home has outdoor areas for resident use and staff help residents go outside.			
The nursing home has an active volunteer program.			
Safety and Care			
The nursing home has an emergency evacuation plan and holds regular fire drills.			
Residents get preventive care, like a yearly flu shot, to help keep them healthy.			
Residents may still see their personal doctors.			
The nursing home has an arrangement with a nearby hospital for emergencies.			
Care plan meetings are held at times that are convenient for residents and family members to attend whenever possible.			
The nursing home has corrected all deficiencies (failure to meet one or more Federal or State requirements) on its last state inspection report.			

Nursing Home Checklist

Additional Comments:

_____

_____

_____

_____

_____

_____

_____

_____

_____

_____

_____

_____

_____

_____

_____

_____

_____

_____

_____

_____

_____

_____

_____

_____

APPENDIX 11:
THE FEDERAL NURSING HOME REFORM
LAW (MEDICAID PROVISION)

U.S.C. TITLE 42, CHAPTER 7, SUBCHAPTER XIX

Sec. 1396r.— Requirements for nursing facilities

(a) "Nursing facility" defined

In this subchapter, the term "nursing facility" means an institution (or a distinct part of an institution) which—

(1) is primarily engaged in providing to residents—

(A) skilled nursing care and related services for residents who require medical or nursing care,

(B) rehabilitation services for the rehabilitation of injured, disabled, or sick persons, or

(C) on a regular basis, health-related care and services to individuals who because of their mental or physical condition require care and services (above the level of room and board) which can be made available to them only through institutional facilities, and is not primarily for the care and treatment of mental diseases;

(2) has in effect a transfer agreement (meeting the requirements of section 1395x(l) of this title) with one or more hospitals having agreements in effect under section 1395cc of this title; and

(3) meets the requirements for a nursing facility described in subsections (b), (c), and (d) of this section.

Such term also includes any facility which is located in a State on an Indian reservation and is certified by the Secretary as meeting the requirements of paragraph (1) and subsections (b), (c), and (d) of this section.

(b) Requirements relating to provision of services

(1) Quality of life

(A) In general

A nursing facility must care for its residents in such a manner and in such an environment as will promote maintenance or enhancement of the quality of life of each resident.

(B) Quality assessment and assurance

A nursing facility must maintain a quality assessment and assurance committee, consisting of the director of nursing services, a physician designated by the facility, and at least 3 other members of the facility's staff, which—

(i) meets at least quarterly to identify issues with respect to which quality assessment and assurance activities are necessary and

(ii) develops and implements appropriate plans of action to correct identified quality deficiencies. A State or the Secretary may not require disclosure of the records of such committee except insofar as such disclosure is related to the compliance of such committee with the requirements of this subparagraph.

(2) Scope of services and activities under plan of care

A nursing facility must provide services and activities to attain or maintain the highest practicable physical, mental, and psychosocial well-being of each resident in accordance with a written plan of care which—

(A) describes the medical, nursing, and psychosocial needs of the resident and how such needs will be met;

(B) is initially prepared, with the participation to the extent practicable of the resident or the resident's family or legal representative, by a team which includes the resident's attending physician and a registered professional nurse with responsibility for the resident; and

(C) is periodically reviewed and revised by such team after each assessment under paragraph (3).

(3) Residents' assessment

(A) Requirement

A nursing facility must conduct a comprehensive, accurate, standardized, reproducible assessment of each resident's functional capacity, which assessment—

(i) describes the resident's capability to perform daily life functions and significant impairments in functional capacity;

(ii) is based on a uniform minimum data set specified by the Secretary under subsection (f)(6)(A) of this section;

(iii) uses an instrument which is specified by the State under subsection (e)(5) of this section; and

(iv) includes the identification of medical problems.

(B) Certification

(i) In general

Each such assessment must be conducted or coordinated (with the appropriate participation of health professionals) by a registered professional nurse who signs and certifies the completion of the assessment. Each individual who completes a portion of such an assessment shall sign and certify as to the accuracy of that portion of the assessment.

(ii) Penalty for falsification

(I) An individual who willfully and knowingly certifies under clause (i) a material and false statement in a resident assessment is subject to a civil money penalty of not more than $1,000 with respect to each assessment.

(II) An individual who willfully and knowingly causes another individual to certify under clause (i) a material and false statement in a resident assessment is subject to a civil money penalty of not more than $5,000 with respect to each assessment.

(III) The provisions of section 1320a-7a of this title (other than subsections (a) and (b)) shall apply to a civil money penalty under this clause in the same manner as such provisions apply to a penalty or proceeding under section 1320a-7a(a) of this title.

(iii) Use of independent assessors

If a State determines, under a survey under subsection (g) of this section or otherwise, that there has been a knowing and willful certification of false assessments under this paragraph, the State may require (for a period specified by the State) that resident assessments under this paragraph be conducted and certified by individuals who are independent of the facility and who are approved by the State.

(C) Frequency

(i) In general

Such an assessment must be conducted—

(I) promptly upon (but no later than 14 days after the date of) admission for each individual admitted on or after October 1, 1990, and by not later than October 1, 1991, for each resident of the facility on that date;

(II) promptly after a significant change in the resident's physical or mental condition; and

(III) in no case less often than once every 12 months.

(ii) Resident review

The nursing facility must examine each resident no less frequently than once every 3 months and, as appropriate, revise the resident's assessment to assure the continuing accuracy of the assessment.

(D) Use

The results of such an assessment shall be used in developing, reviewing, and revising the resident's plan of care under paragraph (2).

(E) Coordination

Such assessments shall be coordinated with any State-required preadmission screening program to the maximum extent practicable in order to avoid duplicative testing and effort. In addition, a nursing facility shall notify the State mental health authority or State mental retardation or developmental disability authority, as applicable, promptly after a significant change in the physical or mental condition of a resident who is mentally ill or mentally retarded.

(F) Requirements relating to preadmission screening for mentally ill and mentally retarded individuals

Except as provided in clauses (ii) and (iii) of subsection (e)(7)(A) of this section, a nursing facility must not admit, on or after January 1, 1989, any new resident who—

(i) is mentally ill (as defined in subsection (e)(7)(G)(i) of this section) unless the State mental health authority has determined (based on an independent physical and mental evaluation performed by a person or entity other than the State mental health authority) prior to admission that, because of the physical and mental condition of the individual, the individual requires the level of services provided by a nursing facility, and, if the individual requires such level of services, whether the individual requires specialized services for mental illness, or

(ii) is mentally retarded (as defined in subsection (e)(7)(G)(ii) of this section) unless the State mental retardation or developmental disability authority has determined prior to admission that, because of the physical and mental condition of the individual, the individual requires the level of services provided by a nursing facility, and, if the individual requires such level of services, whether the individual requires specialized services for mental retardation.

A State mental health authority and a State mental retardation or developmental disability authority may not delegate (by subcontract or otherwise) their responsibilities under this subparagraph to a nursing facility (or to an entity that has a direct or indirect affiliation or relationship with such a facility).

(4) Provision of services and activities

(A) In general

To the extent needed to fulfill all plans of care described in paragraph (2), a nursing facility must provide (or arrange for the provision of)—

(i) nursing and related services and specialized rehabilitative services to attain or maintain the highest practicable physical, mental, and psychosocial well-being of each resident;

(ii) medically-related social services to attain or maintain the highest practicable physical, mental, and psychosocial well-being of each resident;

(iii) pharmaceutical services (including procedures that assure the accurate acquiring, receiving, dispensing, and administering of all drugs and biologicals) to meet the needs of each resident;

(iv) dietary services that assure that the meals meet the daily nutritional and special dietary needs of each resident;

(v) an on-going program, directed by a qualified professional, of activities designed to meet the interests and the physical, mental, and psychosocial well-being of each resident;

(vi) routine dental services (to the extent covered under the State plan) and emergency dental services to meet the needs of each resident; and

(vii) treatment and services required by mentally ill and mentally retarded residents not otherwise provided or arranged for (or required to be provided or arranged for) by the State.

The services provided or arranged by the facility must meet professional standards of quality.

(B) Qualified persons providing services

Services described in clauses (i), (ii), (iii), (iv), and (vi) of subparagraph (A) must be provided by qualified persons in accordance with each resident's written plan of care.

(C) Required nursing care; facility waivers

(i) General requirements

With respect to nursing facility services provided on or after October 1, 1990, a nursing facility—

(I) except as provided in clause (ii), must provide 24-hour licensed nursing services which are sufficient to meet the nursing needs of its residents, and

(II) except as provided in clause (ii), must use the services of a registered professional nurse for at least 8 consecutive hours a day, 7 days a week.

(ii) Waiver by State

To the extent that a facility is unable to meet the requirements of clause (i), a State may waive such requirements with respect to the facility if—

(I) the facility demonstrates to the satisfaction of the State that the facility has been unable, despite diligent efforts (including offering wages at the community prevailing rate for nursing facilities), to recruit appropriate personnel,

(II) the State determines that a waiver of the requirement will not endanger the health or safety of individuals staying in the facility,

(III) the State finds that, for any such periods in which licensed nursing services are not available, a registered professional nurse or a physician is obligated to respond immediately to telephone calls from the facility,

(IV) the State agency granting a waiver of such requirements provides notice of the waiver to the State long-term care ombudsman (established under section 307(a)(12) [1] of the

Older Americans Act of 1965) and the protection and advocacy system in the State for the mentally ill and the mentally retarded, and

(V) the nursing facility that is granted such a waiver by a State notifies residents of the facility (or, where appropriate, the guardians or legal representatives of such residents) and members of their immediate families of the waiver. A waiver under this clause shall be subject to annual review and to the review of the Secretary and subject to clause (iii) shall be accepted by the Secretary for purposes of this subchapter to the same extent as is the State's certification of the facility. In granting or renewing a waiver, a State may require the facility to use other qualified, licensed personnel.

(iii) Assumption of waiver authority by Secretary

If the Secretary determines that a State has shown a clear pattern and practice of allowing waivers in the absence of diligent efforts by facilities to meet the staffing requirements, the Secretary shall assume and exercise the authority of the State to grant waivers.

(5) Required training of nurse aides

(A) In general

(i) Except as provided in clause (ii), a nursing facility must not use on a full-time basis any individual as a nurse aide in the facility on or after October 1, 1990, for more than 4 months unless the individual—

(I) has completed a training and competency evaluation program, or a competency evaluation program, approved by the State under subsection (e)(1)(A) of this section, and

(II) is competent to provide nursing or nursing-related services.

(ii) A nursing facility must not use on a temporary, per diem, leased, or on any other basis other than as a permanent employee any individual as a nurse aide in the facility on or after January 1, 1991, unless the individual meets the requirements described in clause (i).

(B) Offering competency evaluation programs for current employees

A nursing facility must provide, for individuals used as a nurse aide by the facility as of January 1, 1990, for a competency evaluation program approved by the State under subsection (e)(1) of this section and such preparation as may be necessary for the individual to complete such a program by October 1, 1990.

(C) Competency

The nursing facility must not permit an individual, other than in a training and competency evaluation program approved by the State, to serve as a nurse aide or provide services of a type for which the individual has not demonstrated competency and must not use such an individual as a nurse aide unless the facility has inquired of any State registry established under subsection (e)(2)(A) of this section that the facility believes will include information concerning the individual.

(D) Re-training required

For purposes of subparagraph (A), if, since an individual's most recent completion of a training and competency evaluation program, there has been a continuous period of 24 consecutive months during none of which the individual performed nursing or nursing-related services for monetary compensation, such individual shall complete a new training and competency evaluation program, or a new competency evaluation program.

(E) Regular in-service education

The nursing facility must provide such regular performance review and regular in-service education as assures that individuals used as nurse aides are competent to perform services as nurse aides, including training for individuals providing nursing and nursing-related services to residents with cognitive impairments.

(F) "Nurse aide" defined

In this paragraph, the term "nurse aide" means any individual providing nursing or nursing-related services to residents in a nursing facility, but does not include an individual—

(i) who is a licensed health professional (as defined in subparagraph (G)) or a registered dietician, or

(ii) who volunteers to provide such services without monetary compensation.

(G) Licensed health professional defined

In this paragraph, the term "licensed health professional" means a physician, physician assistant, nurse practitioner, physical, speech, or occupational therapist, physical or occupational therapy assistant, registered professional nurse, licensed practical nurse, or licensed or certified social worker.

(6) Physician supervision and clinical records

A nursing facility must—

(A) require that the health care of every resident be provided under the supervision of a physician (or, at the option of a State, under the supervision of a nurse practitioner, clinical nurse specialist, or physician assistant who is not an employee of the facility but who is working in collaboration with a physician);

(B) provide for having a physician available to furnish necessary medical care in case of emergency; and

(C) maintain clinical records on all residents, which records include the plans of care (described in paragraph (2)) and the residents' assessments (described in paragraph (3)), as well as the results of any pre-admission screening conducted under subsection (e)(7) of this section.

(7) Required social services

In the case of a nursing facility with more than 120 beds, the facility must have at least one social worker (with at least a bachelor's degree in social work or similar professional qualifications) employed full-time to provide or assure the provision of social services.

(c) Requirements relating to residents' rights

(1) General rights

(A) Specified rights

A nursing facility must protect and promote the rights of each resident, including each of the following rights:

(i) Free choice

The right to choose a personal attending physician, to be fully informed in advance about care and treatment, to be fully informed in advance of any changes in care or treatment that may affect the resident's well-being, and (except with respect to a resident adjudged incompetent) to participate in planning care and treatment or changes in care and treatment.

(ii) Free from restraints

The right to be free from physical or mental abuse, corporal punishment, involuntary seclusion, and any physical or chemical restraints imposed for purposes of discipline or convenience and not required to treat the resident's medical symptoms. Restraints may only be imposed—

(I) to ensure the physical safety of the resident or other residents, and

(II) only upon the written order of a physician that specifies the duration and circumstances under which the restraints are to be used (except in emergency circumstances specified by the Secretary until such an order could reasonably be obtained).

(iii) Privacy

The right to privacy with regard to accommodations, medical treatment, written and telephonic communications, visits, and meetings of family and of resident groups.

(iv) Confidentiality

The right to confidentiality of personal and clinical records and to access to current clinical records of the resident upon request by the resident or the resident's legal representative, within 24 hours (excluding hours occurring during a weekend or holiday) after making such a request.

(v) Accommodation of needs

The right—

(I) to reside and receive services with reasonable accommodation of individual needs and preferences, except where the health or safety of the individual or other residents would be endangered, and

(II) to receive notice before the room or roommate of the resident in the facility is changed.

(vi) Grievances

The right to voice grievances with respect to treatment or care that is (or fails to be) furnished, without discrimination or reprisal for voicing the grievances and the right to prompt efforts by the facility to resolve grievances the resident may have, including those with respect to the behavior of other residents.

(vii) Participation in resident and family groups

The right of the resident to organize and participate in resident groups in the facility and the right of the resident's family to meet in the facility with the families of other residents in the facility.

(viii) Participation in other activities

The right of the resident to participate in social, religious, and community activities that do not interfere with the rights of other residents in the facility.

(ix) Examination of survey results

The right to examine, upon reasonable request, the results of the most recent survey of the facility conducted by the Secretary or a State with respect to the facility and any plan of correction in effect with respect to the facility.

(x) Refusal of certain transfers

The right to refuse a transfer to another room within the facility, if a purpose of the transfer is to relocate the resident from a portion of the facility that is not a skilled nursing facility (for purposes of subchapter XVIII of this chapter) to a portion of the facility that is such a skilled nursing facility.

(xi) Other rights

Any other right established by the Secretary.

Clause (iii) shall not be construed as requiring the provision of a private room. A resident's exercise of a right to refuse transfer under clause (x) shall not affect the resident's eligibility or entitlement to medical assistance under this subchapter or a State's entitlement to Federal medical assistance under this subchapter with respect to services furnished to such a resident.

(B) Notice of rights

A nursing facility must—

(i) inform each resident, orally and in writing at the time of admission to the facility, of the resident's legal rights during the stay at the facility and of the requirements and procedures for establishing eligibility for medical assistance under this subchapter, including the right to request an assessment under section 1396r-5(c)(1)(B) of this title;

(ii) make available to each resident, upon reasonable request, a written statement of such rights (which statement is updated upon changes in such rights) including the notice (if any) of the State developed under subsection (e)(6) of this section;

(iii) inform each resident who is entitled to medical assistance under this subchapter—

(I) at the time of admission to the facility or, if later, at the time the resident becomes eligible for such assistance, of the items and services (including those specified under section 1396a(a)(28)(B) of this title) that are included in nursing facility services under the State plan and for which the resident may not be charged (except as permitted in section 1396o of this title), and of those other items and services that the facility offers and for which the resident may be charged and the amount of the charges for such items and services, and

(II) of changes in the items and services described in subclause (I) and of changes in the charges imposed for items and services described in that subclause; and

(iv) inform each other resident, in writing before or at the time of admission and periodically during the resident's stay, of services available in the facility and of related charges for such services, including any charges for services not covered under subchapter XVIII of this chapter or by the facility's basic per diem charge.

The written description of legal rights under this subparagraph shall include a description of the protection of personal funds under paragraph (6) and a statement that a resident may file a complaint with a State survey and certification agency respecting resident abuse and neglect and misappropriation of resident property in the facility.

(C) Rights of incompetent residents

In the case of a resident adjudged incompetent under the laws of a State, the rights of the resident under this subchapter shall devolve upon, and, to the extent judged necessary by a court of competent jurisdiction, be exercised by, the person appointed under State law to act on the resident's behalf.

(D) Use of psychopharmacologic drugs

Psychopharmacologic drugs may be administered only on the orders of a physician and only as part of a plan (included in the written plan of care described in paragraph (2)) designed to eliminate or modify the symptoms for which the drugs are prescribed and only if, at least annually an independent, external consultant reviews the appropriateness of the drug plan of each resident receiving such drugs.

(2) Transfer and discharge rights

(A) In general

A nursing facility must permit each resident to remain in the facility and must not transfer or discharge the resident from the facility unless—

(i) the transfer or discharge is necessary to meet the resident's welfare and the resident's welfare cannot be met in the facility;

(ii) the transfer or discharge is appropriate because the resident's health has improved sufficiently so the resident no longer needs the services provided by the facility;

(iii) the safety of individuals in the facility is endangered;

(iv) the health of individuals in the facility would otherwise be endangered;

(v) the resident has failed, after reasonable and appropriate notice, to pay (or to have paid under this subchapter or subchapter XVIII of this chapter on the resident's behalf) for a stay at the facility; or

(vi) the facility ceases to operate.

In each of the cases described in clauses (i) through (iv), the basis for the transfer or discharge must be documented in the resident's clinical record. In the cases described in clauses (i) and (ii), the documentation must be made by the resident's physician, and in the case described in clause (iv) the documentation must be made by a physician. For purposes of clause (v), in the case of a resident who becomes eligible for assistance under this subchapter after admission to the facility, only charges which may be imposed under this subchapter shall be considered to be allowable.

(B) Pre-transfer and pre-discharge notice

(i) In general

Before effecting a transfer or discharge of a resident, a nursing facility must—

(I) notify the resident (and, if known, an immediate family member of the resident or legal representative) of the transfer or discharge and the reasons therefor,

(II) record the reasons in the resident's clinical record (including any documentation required under subparagraph (A)), and

(III) include in the notice the items described in clause (iii).

(ii) Timing of notice

The notice under clause (i)(I) must be made at least 30 days in advance of the resident's transfer or discharge except—

(I) in a case described in clause (iii) or (iv) of subparagraph (A);

(II) in a case described in clause (ii) of subparagraph (A), where the resident's health improves sufficiently to allow a more immediate transfer or discharge;

(III) in a case described in clause (i) of subparagraph (A), where a more immediate transfer or discharge is necessitated by the resident's urgent medical needs; or

(IV) in a case where a resident has not resided in the facility for 30 days. In the case of such exceptions, notice must be given as many days before the date of the transfer or discharge as is practicable.

(iii) Items included in notice

Each notice under clause (i) must include—

(I) for transfers or discharges effected on or after October 1, 1989, notice of the resident's right to appeal the transfer or discharge under the State process established under subsection (e)(3) of this section;

(II) the name, mailing address, and telephone number of the State long-term care ombudsman (established under title III or VII of the Older Americans Act of 1965 (42 U.S.C. 3021 et seq., 3058 et seq.) in accordance with section 712 of the Act (42 U.S.C. 3058g));

(III) in the case of residents with developmental disabilities, the mailing address and telephone number of the agency responsible for the protection and advocacy system for developmentally disabled individuals established under subtitle C of the Developmental Disabilities Assistance and Bill of Rights Act of 2000 (42 U.S.C. 15041 et seq.); and

(IV) in the case of mentally ill residents (as defined in subsection (e)(7)(G)(i) of this section), the mailing address and telephone number of the agency responsible for the protection and advocacy system for mentally ill individuals established under the Protection and Advocacy for Mentally Ill Individuals Act [2] (42 U.S.C. 10801 et seq.).

(C) Orientation

A nursing facility must provide sufficient preparation and orientation to residents to ensure safe and orderly transfer or discharge from the facility.

(D) Notice on bed-hold policy and readmission

(i) Notice before transfer

Before a resident of a nursing facility is transferred for hospitalization or therapeutic leave, a nursing facility must provide written information to the resident and an immediate family member or legal representative concerning—

(I) the provisions of the State plan under this subchapter regarding the period (if any) during which the resident will be permitted under the State plan to return and resume residence in the facility, and

(II) the policies of the facility regarding such a period, which policies must be consistent with clause (iii).

(ii) Notice upon transfer

At the time of transfer of a resident to a hospital or for therapeutic leave, a nursing facility must provide written notice to the resident and an immediate family member or legal representative of the duration of any period described in clause (i).

(iii) Permitting resident to return

A nursing facility must establish and follow a written policy under which a resident—

(I) who is eligible for medical assistance for nursing facility services under a State plan,

(II) who is transferred from the facility for hospitalization or therapeutic leave, and

(III) whose hospitalization or therapeutic leave exceeds a period paid for under the State plan for the holding of a bed in the facility for the resident, will be permitted to be readmitted to the facility immediately upon the first availability of a bed in a semiprivate room in the facility if, at the time of readmission, the resident requires the services provided by the facility.

(E) Information respecting advance directives

A nursing facility must comply with the requirement of section 1396a(w) of this title (relating to maintaining written policies and procedures respecting advance directives).

(F) Continuing rights in case of voluntary withdrawal from participation

(i) In general

In the case of a nursing facility that voluntarily withdraws from participation in a State plan under this subchapter but continues to provide services of the type provided by nursing facilities—

(I) the facility's voluntary withdrawal from participation is not an acceptable basis for the transfer or discharge of residents of the facility who were residing in the facility on the day before the effective date of the withdrawal (including those residents who were not entitled to medical assistance as of such day);

(II) the provisions of this section continue to apply to such residents until the date of their discharge from the facility; and

(III) in the case of each individual who begins residence in the facility after the effective date of such withdrawal, the facility shall provide notice orally and in a prominent manner in writing on a separate page at the time the individual begins residence of the information described in clause (ii) and shall obtain from each such individual at such time an acknowledgment of receipt of such information that is in writing, signed by the individual, and separate from other documents signed by such individual. Nothing in this subparagraph shall be construed as affecting any requirement of a participation agreement that a nursing facility provide advance notice to the State or the Secretary, or both, of its intention to terminate the agreement.

(ii) Information for new residents

The information described in this clause for a resident is the following:

(I) The facility is not participating in the program under this subchapter with respect to that resident.

THE FEDERAL NURSING HOME REFORM LAW (MEDICAID PROVISION)

(II) The facility may transfer or discharge the resident from the facility at such time as the resident is unable to pay the charges of the facility, even though the resident may have become eligible for medical assistance for nursing facility services under this subchapter.

(iii) Continuation of payments and oversight authority

Notwithstanding any other provision of this subchapter, with respect to the residents described in clause (i)(I), a participation agreement of a facility described in clause (i) is deemed to continue in effect under such plan after the effective date of the facility's voluntary withdrawal from participation under the State plan for purposes of—

(I) receiving payments under the State plan for nursing facility services provided to such residents;

(II) maintaining compliance with all applicable requirements of this subchapter; and

(III) continuing to apply the survey, certification, and enforcement authority provided under subsections (g) and (h) of this section (including involuntary termination of a participation agreement deemed continued under this clause).

(iv) No application to new residents

This paragraph (other than subclause (III) of clause (i)) shall not apply to an individual who begins residence in a facility on or after the effective date of the withdrawal from participation under this subparagraph.

(3) Access and visitation rights

A nursing facility must—

(A) permit immediate access to any resident by any representative of the Secretary, by any representative of the State, by an ombudsman or agency described in subclause (II), (III), or (IV) of paragraph (2)(B)(iii), or by the resident's individual physician;

(B) permit immediate access to a resident, subject to the resident's right to deny or withdraw consent at any time, by immediate family or other relatives of the resident;

(C) permit immediate access to a resident, subject to reasonable restrictions and the resident's right to deny or withdraw consent at any time, by others who are visiting with the consent of the resident;

(D) permit reasonable access to a resident by any entity or individual that provides health, social, legal, or other services to the resident, subject to the resident's right to deny or withdraw consent at any time; and

(E) permit representatives of the State ombudsman (described in paragraph (2)(B)(iii)(II)), with the permission of the resident (or the resident's legal representative) and consistent with State law, to examine a resident's clinical records.

(4) Equal access to quality care

(A) In general

A nursing facility must establish and maintain identical policies and practices regarding transfer, discharge, and the provision of services required under the State plan for all individuals regardless of source of payment.

(B) Construction

(i) Nothing prohibiting any charges for non-medicaid patients

Subparagraph (A) shall not be construed as prohibiting a nursing facility from charging any amount for services furnished, consistent with the notice in paragraph (1)(B) describing such charges.

(ii) No additional services required

Subparagraph (A) shall not be construed as requiring a State to offer additional services on behalf of a resident than are otherwise provided under the State plan.

(5) Admissions policy

(A) Admissions

With respect to admissions practices, a nursing facility must—

(i) (I) not require individuals applying to reside or residing in the facility to waive their rights to benefits under this subchapter or subchapter XVIII of this chapter,

(II) not require oral or written assurance that such individuals are not eligible for, or will not apply for, benefits under this subchapter or subchapter XVIII of this chapter, and

(III) prominently display in the facility written information, and provide to such individuals oral and written information, about how to apply for and use such benefits and how to receive refunds for previous payments covered by such benefits;

(ii) not require a third party guarantee of payment to the facility as a condition of admission (or expedited admission) to, or continued stay in, the facility; and

(iii) in the case of an individual who is entitled to medical assistance for nursing facility services, not charge, solicit, accept, or receive, in addition to any amount otherwise required to be paid under the State plan under this subchapter, any gift, money, donation, or other consideration as a precondition of admitting (or expediting the admission of) the individual to the facility or as a requirement for the individual's continued stay in the facility.

(B) Construction

(i) No preemption of stricter standards

Subparagraph (A) shall not be construed as preventing States or political subdivisions therein from prohibiting, under State or local law, the discrimination against individuals who are entitled to medical assistance under the State plan with respect to admissions practices of nursing facilities.

(ii) Contracts with legal representatives

Subparagraph (A)(ii) shall not be construed as preventing a facility from requiring an individual, who has legal access to a resident's income or resources available to pay for care in the facility, to sign a contract (without incurring personal financial liability) to provide payment from the resident's income or resources for such care.

(iii) Charges for additional services requested

Subparagraph (A)(iii) shall not be construed as preventing a facility from charging a resident, eligible for medical assistance under the State plan, for items or services the resident has requested and received and that are not specified in the State plan as included in the term "nursing facility services".

(iv) Bona fide contributions

Subparagraph (A)(iii) shall not be construed as prohibiting a nursing facility from soliciting, accepting, or receiving a charitable, religious, or philanthropic contribution from an organization or from a person unrelated to the resident (or potential resident), but only to the extent that such contribution is not a condition of admission, expediting admission, or continued stay in the facility.

(6) Protection of resident funds

(A) In general

The nursing facility—

(i) may not require residents to deposit their personal funds with the facility, and

(ii) upon the written authorization of the resident, must hold, safeguard, and account for such personal funds under a system established and maintained by the facility in accordance with this paragraph.

(B) Management of personal funds

Upon written authorization of a resident under subparagraph (A)(ii), the facility must manage and account for the personal funds of the resident deposited with the facility as follows:

(i) Deposit

The facility must deposit any amount of personal funds in excess of $50 with respect to a resident in an interest bearing account (or accounts) that is separate from any of the facility's operating accounts and credits all interest earned on such separate account to such account. With respect to any other personal funds, the facility must maintain such funds in a non-interest bearing account or petty cash fund.

(ii) Accounting and records

The facility must assure a full and complete separate accounting of each such resident's personal funds, maintain a written record of all financial transactions involving the personal funds of a resident deposited with the facility, and afford the resident (or a legal representative of the resident) reasonable access to such record.

(iii) Notice of certain balances

The facility must notify each resident receiving medical assistance under the State plan under this subchapter when the amount in the resident's account reaches $200 less than the dollar amount determined under section 1382(a)(3)(B) of this title and the fact that if the amount in the account (in addition to the value of the resident's other nonexempt resources) reaches the amount determined under such section the resident may lose eligibility for such medical assistance or for benefits under subchapter XVI of this chapter.

(iv) Conveyance upon death

Upon the death of a resident with such an account, the facility must convey promptly the resident's personal funds (and a final accounting of such funds) to the individual administering the resident's estate.

(C) Assurance of financial security

The facility must purchase a surety bond, or otherwise provide assurance satisfactory to the Secretary, to assure the security of all personal funds of residents deposited with the facility.

(D) Limitation on charges to personal funds

The facility may not impose a charge against the personal funds of a resident for any item or service for which payment is made under this subchapter or subchapter XVIII of this chapter.

(7) Limitation on charges in case of medicaid-eligible individuals

(A) In general

A nursing facility may not impose charges, for certain medicaid-eligible individuals for nursing facility services covered by the State under its plan under this subchapter, that exceed the payment amounts established by the State for such services under this subchapter.

(B) "Certain medicaid-eligible individual" defined

In subparagraph (A), the term "certain medicaid-eligible individual" means an individual who is entitled to medical assistance for nursing facility services in the facility under this subchapter but with respect to whom such benefits are not being paid because, in determining the amount of the individual's income to be applied monthly to payment for the costs of such services, the amount of such income exceeds the payment amounts established by the State for such services under this subchapter.

(8) Posting of survey results

A nursing facility must post in a place readily accessible to residents, and family members and legal representatives of residents, the results of the most recent survey of the facility conducted under subsection (g) of this section.

(d) Requirements relating to administration and other matters

(1) Administration

(A) In general

A nursing facility must be administered in a manner that enables it to use its resources effectively and efficiently to attain or maintain the highest practicable physical, mental, and psychosocial well-being of each resident (consistent with requirements established under subsection (f)(5) of this section).

(B) Required notices

If a change occurs in—

(i) the persons with an ownership or control interest (as defined in section 1320a-3(a)(3) of this title) in the facility,

(ii) the persons who are officers, directors, agents, or managing employees (as defined in section 1320a-5(b) of this title) of the facility,

(iii) the corporation, association, or other company responsible for the management of the facility, or

(iv) the individual who is the administrator or director of nursing of the facility,

the nursing facility must provide notice to the State agency responsible for the licensing of the facility, at the time of the change, of the change and of the identity of each new person, company, or individual described in the respective clause.

(C) Nursing facility administrator

The administrator of a nursing facility must meet standards established by the Secretary under subsection (f)(4) of this section.

(2) Licensing and Life Safety Code

(A) Licensing

A nursing facility must be licensed under applicable State and local law.

(B) Life Safety Code

A nursing facility must meet such provisions of such edition (as specified by the Secretary in regulation) of the Life Safety Code of the National Fire Protection Association as are applicable to nursing homes; except that—

(i) the Secretary may waive, for such periods as he deems appropriate, specific provisions of such Code which if rigidly applied would result in unreasonable hardship upon a facility, but only if such waiver would not adversely affect the health and safety of residents or personnel, and

(ii) the provisions of such Code shall not apply in any State if the Secretary finds that in such State there is in effect a fire and safety code, imposed by State law, which adequately protects residents of and personnel in nursing facilities.

(3) Sanitary and infection control and physical environment

A nursing facility must—

(A) establish and maintain an infection control program designed to provide a safe, sanitary, and comfortable environment in which residents reside and to help prevent the development and transmission of disease and infection, and

(B) be designed, constructed, equipped, and maintained in a manner to protect the health and safety of residents, personnel, and the general public.

(4) Miscellaneous

(A) Compliance with Federal, State, and local laws and professional standards

A nursing facility must operate and provide services in compliance with all applicable Federal, State, and local laws and regulations (including the requirements of section 1320a-3 of this title) and with accepted professional standards and principles which apply to professionals providing services in such a facility.

(B) Other

A nursing facility must meet such other requirements relating to the health and safety of residents or relating to the physical facilities thereof as the Secretary may find necessary.

(e) State requirements relating to nursing facility requirements

As a condition of approval of its plan under this subchapter, a State must provide for the following:

(1) Specification and review of nurse aide training and competency evaluation programs and of nurse aide competency evaluation programs

The State must—

(A) by not later than January 1, 1989, specify those training and competency evaluation programs, and those competency evaluation programs, that the State approves for purposes of subsection (b)(5) of this section and that meet the requirements established under subsection (f)(2) of this section, and

(B) by not later than January 1, 1990, provide for the review and reapproval of such programs, at a frequency and using a methodology consistent with the requirements established under subsection (f)(2)(A)(iii) of this section.

The failure of the Secretary to establish requirements under subsection (f)(2) of this section shall not relieve any State of its responsibility under this paragraph.

(2) Nurse aide registry

(A) In general

By not later than January 1, 1989, the State shall establish and maintain a registry of all individuals who have satisfactorily completed a nurse aide training and competency evaluation program, or a nurse aide competency evaluation program, approved under paragraph (1) in the State, or any individual described in subsection (f)(2)(B)(ii) of this section or in subparagraph (B), (C), or (D) of section 6901(b)(4) of the Omnibus Budget Reconciliation Act of 1989.

(B) Information in registry

The registry under subparagraph (A) shall provide (in accordance with regulations of the Secretary) for the inclusion of specific documented findings by a State under subsection (g)(1)(C) of this section of resident neglect or abuse or misappropriation of resident property involving an individual listed in the registry, as well as any brief statement of the individual disputing the findings. The State shall make available to the public information in the registry. In the case of inquiries to the registry concerning an individual listed in the registry, any information disclosed concerning such a finding shall also include disclosure of any such statement in the registry relating to the finding or a clear and accurate summary of such a statement.

(C) Prohibition against charges

A State may not impose any charges on a nurse aide relating to the registry established and maintained under subparagraph (A).

(3) State appeals process for transfers and discharges

The State, for transfers and discharges from nursing facilities effected on or after October 1, 1989, must provide for a fair mechanism, meeting the guidelines established under subsection (f)(3) of this section, for hearing appeals on transfers and discharges of residents of such facilities; but the failure of the Secretary to establish such guidelines under such subsection shall not relieve any State of its responsibility under this paragraph.

(4) Nursing facility administrator standards

By not later than July 1, 1989, the State must have implemented and enforced the nursing facility administrator standards developed under subsection (f)(4) of this section respecting the qualification of administrators of nursing facilities.

(5) Specification of resident assessment instrument

Effective July 1, 1990, the State shall specify the instrument to be used by nursing facilities in the State in complying with the requirement of subsection (b)(3)(A)(iii) of this section. Such instrument shall be—

(A) one of the instruments designated under subsection (f)(6)(B) of this section, or

(B) an instrument which the Secretary has approved as being consistent with the minimum data set of core elements, common definitions, and utilization guidelines specified by the Secretary under subsection (f)(6)(A) of this section.

(6) Notice of medicaid rights

Each State, as a condition of approval of its plan under this subchapter, effective April 1, 1988, must develop (and periodically update) a written notice of the rights and obligations of residents of nursing facilities (and spouses of such residents) under this subchapter.

(7) State requirements for preadmission screening and resident review

(A) Preadmission screening

(i) In general

Effective January 1, 1989, the State must have in effect a preadmission screening program, for making determinations (using any criteria developed under subsection (f)(8) of this section) described in subsection (b)(3)(F) of this section for mentally ill and mentally retarded individuals (as defined in subparagraph (G)) who are admitted to nursing facilities on or after January 1, 1989. The failure of the Secretary to develop minimum criteria under subsection (f)(8) of this section shall not relieve any State of its responsibility to have a preadmission screening program under this subparagraph or to perform resident reviews under subparagraph (B).

(ii) Clarification with respect to certain readmissions

The preadmission screening program under clause (i) need not provide for determinations in the case of the readmission to a nursing facility of an individual who, after being admitted to the nursing facility, was transferred for care in a hospital.

(iii) Exception for certain hospital discharges

The preadmission screening program under clause (i) shall not apply to the admission to a nursing facility of an individual—

(I) who is admitted to the facility directly from a hospital after receiving acute inpatient care at the hospital,

(II) who requires nursing facility services for the condition for which the individual received care in the hospital, and

(III) whose attending physician has certified, before admission to the facility, that the individual is likely to require less than 30 days of nursing facility services.

(B) State requirement for resident review

(i) For mentally ill residents

As of April 1, 1990, in the case of each resident of a nursing facility who is mentally ill, the State mental health authority must review and determine (using any criteria developed under subsection (f)(8) of this section and based on an independent physical and mental evaluation performed by a person or entity other than the State mental health authority)—

(I) whether or not the resident, because of the resident's physical and mental condition, requires the level of services provided by a nursing facility or requires the level of services of an inpatient psychiatric hospital for individuals under age 21 (as described in section 1396d(h) of this title) or of an institution for mental diseases providing medical assistance to individuals 65 years of age or older; and

(II) whether or not the resident requires specialized services for mental illness.

(ii) For mentally retarded residents

As of April 1, 1990, in the case of each resident of a nursing facility who is mentally retarded, the State mental retardation or developmental disability authority must review and determine (using any criteria developed under subsection (f)(8) of this section)—

(I) whether or not the resident, because of the resident's physical and mental condition, requires the level of services provided by a nursing facility or requires the level of services of an intermediate care facility described under section 1396d(d) of this title; and

(II) whether or not the resident requires specialized services for mental retardation.

(iii) Review required upon change in resident's condition

A review and determination under clause (i) or (ii) must be conducted promptly after a nursing facility has notified the State mental health authority or State mental retardation or developmental disability authority, as applicable, under subsection (b)(3)(E) of this section with respect to a mentally ill or mentally retarded resident, that there has been a significant change in the resident's physical or mental condition.

(iv) Prohibition of delegation

A State mental health authority, a State mental retardation or developmental disability authority, and a State may not delegate (by subcontract or otherwise) their responsibilities under this subparagraph to a nursing facility (or to an entity that has a direct or indirect affiliation or relationship with such a facility).

(C) Response to preadmission screening and resident review

As of April 1, 1990, the State must meet the following requirements:

(i) Long-term residents not requiring nursing facility services, but requiring specialized services

In the case of a resident who is determined, under subparagraph (B), not to require the level of services provided by a nursing facility, but to require specialized services for mental illness or mental retardation, and who has continuously resided in a nursing facility for at least 30 months before the date of the determination, the State must, in consultation with the resident's family or legal representative and care-givers—

(I) inform the resident of the institutional and noninstitutional alternatives covered under the State plan for the resident,

(II) offer the resident the choice of remaining in the facility or of receiving covered services in an alternative appropriate institutional or noninstitutional setting,

(III) clarify the effect on eligibility for services under the State plan if the resident chooses to leave the facility (including its effect on readmission to the facility), and

(IV) regardless of the resident's choice, provide for (or arrange for the provision of) such specialized services for the mental illness or mental retardation. A State shall not be denied payment under this subchapter for nursing facility services for a resident described in this clause because the resident does not require the level of services provided by such a facility, if the resident chooses to remain in such a facility.

(ii) Other residents not requiring nursing facility services, but requiring specialized services

In the case of a resident who is determined, under subparagraph (B), not to require the level of services provided by a nursing facility, but to require specialized services for mental illness or mental retardation, and who has not continuously resided in a nursing facility for at least 30 months before the date of the determination, the State must, in consultation with the resident's family or legal representative and care-givers—

(I) arrange for the safe and orderly discharge of the resident from the facility, consistent with the requirements of subsection (c)(2) of this section,

(II) prepare and orient the resident for such discharge, and

(III) provide for (or arrange for the provision of) such specialized services for the mental illness or mental retardation.

(iii) Residents not requiring nursing facility services and not requiring specialized services

In the case of a resident who is determined, under subparagraph (B), not to require the level of services provided by a nursing facility and not to require specialized services for mental illness or mental retardation, the State must—

(I) arrange for the safe and orderly discharge of the resident from the facility, consistent with the requirements of subsection (c)(2) of this section, and

(II) prepare and orient the resident for such discharge.

(iv) Annual report

Each State shall report to the Secretary annually concerning the number and disposition of residents described in each of clauses (ii) and (iii).

(D) Denial of payment

(i) For failure to conduct preadmission screening or review

No payment may be made under section 1396b(a) of this title with respect to nursing facility services furnished to an individual for whom a determination is required under subsection (b)(3)(F) of this section or subparagraph (B) but for whom the determination is not made.

(ii) For certain residents not requiring nursing facility level of services

No payment may be made under section 1396b(a) of this title with respect to nursing facility services furnished to an individual (other than an individual described in subparagraph (C)(i)) who does not require the level of services provided by a nursing facility.

(E) Permitting alternative disposition plans

With respect to residents of a nursing facility who are mentally retarded or mentally ill and who are determined under subparagraph (B) not to require the level of services of such a facility, but who require specialized services for mental illness or mental retardation, a State and the nursing facility shall be considered to be in compliance with the requirements of subparagraphs (A) through (C) of this paragraph if, before April 1, 1989, the State and the Secretary have entered into an agreement relating to the disposition of such residents of the facility and the State is in compliance with such agreement. Such an agreement may provide for the disposition of the residents after the date specified in subparagraph (C). The State may revise such an agreement, subject to the approval of the Secretary, before October 1, 1991, but only if, under the revised agreement, all residents subject to the agreement who do not require the level of services of such a facility are discharged from the facility by not later than April 1, 1994.

(F) Appeals procedures

Each State, as a condition of approval of its plan under this subchapter, effective January 1, 1989, must have in effect an appeals process for individuals adversely affected by determinations under subparagraph (A) or (B).

(G) Definitions

In this paragraph and in subsection (b)(3)(F) of this section:

(i) An individual is considered to be "mentally ill" if the individual has a serious mental illness (as defined by the Secretary in consultation with the National Institute of Mental Health) and does not have a primary diagnosis of dementia (including Alzheimer's disease or a related disorder) or a diagnosis (other than a primary diagnosis) of dementia and a primary diagnosis that is not a serious mental illness.

(ii) An individual is considered to be "mentally retarded" if the individual is mentally retarded or a person with a related condition (as described in section 1396d(d) of this title).

(iii) The term "specialized services" has the meaning given such term by the Secretary in regulations, but does not include, in the case of a resident of a nursing facility, services within the scope of services which the facility must provide or arrange for its residents under subsection (b)(4) of this section.

(f) Responsibilities of Secretary relating to nursing facility requirements

(1) General responsibility

It is the duty and responsibility of the Secretary to assure that requirements which govern the provision of care in nursing facilities under State plans approved under this subchapter, and the enforcement of such requirements, are adequate to protect the health, safety, welfare, and rights of residents and to promote the effective and efficient use of public moneys.

(2) Requirements for nurse aide training and competency evaluation programs and for nurse aide competency evaluation programs

(A) In general

For purposes of subsections (b)(5) and (e)(1)(A) of this section, the Secretary shall establish, by not later than September 1, 1988—

(i) requirements for the approval of nurse aide training and competency evaluation programs, including requirements relating to

(I) the areas to be covered in such a program (including at least basic nursing skills, personal care skills, recognition of mental health and social service needs, care of cognitively impaired residents, basic restorative services, and residents' rights) and content of the curriculum,

(II) minimum hours of initial and ongoing training and retraining (including not less than 75 hours in the case of initial training),

(III) qualifications of instructors, and

(IV) procedures for determination of competency;

(ii) requirements for the approval of nurse aide competency evaluation programs, including requirement relating to the areas to be covered in such a program, including at least basic nursing skills, personal care skills, recognition of mental health and social service needs, care of cognitively impaired residents, basic restorative services, and residents' rights, and procedures for determination of competency;

(iii) requirements respecting the minimum frequency and methodology to be used by a State in reviewing such programs' compliance with the requirements for such programs; and

(iv) requirements, under both such programs, that—

(I) provide procedures for determining competency that permit a nurse aide, at the nurse aide's option, to establish competency through procedures or methods other than the passing of a written examination and to have the competency evaluation conducted at the nursing facility at which the aide is (or will be) employed (unless the facility is described in subparagraph (B)(iii)(I)),

(II) prohibit the imposition on a nurse aide who is employed by (or who has received an offer of employment from) a facility on the date on which the aide begins either such program of any charges (including any charges for textbooks and other required course materials and any charges for the competency evaluation) for either such program, and

(III) in the case of a nurse aide not described in subclause (II) who is employed by (or who has received an offer of employment from) a facility not later than 12 months after completing either such program, the State shall provide for the reimbursement of costs incurred in completing such program on a prorata basis during the period in which the nurse aide is so employed.

(B) Approval of certain programs

Such requirements—

(i) may permit approval of programs offered by or in facilities, as well as outside facilities (including employee organizations), and of programs in effect on December 22, 1987;

(ii) shall permit a State to find that an individual who has completed (before July 1, 1989) a nurse aide training and competency evaluation program shall be deemed to have completed such a program approved under subsection (b)(5) of this section if the State determines that, at the time the program was offered, the program met the requirements for approval under such paragraph; and

(iii) subject to subparagraph (C), shall prohibit approval of such a program—

(I) offered by or in a nursing facility which, within the previous 2 years—

(a) has operated under a waiver under subsection (b)(4)(C)(ii) of this section that was granted on the basis of a demonstration that the facility is unable to provide the nursing care required under subsection (b)(4)(C)(i) of this section for a period in excess of 48 hours during a week;

(b) has been subject to an extended (or partial extended) survey under section 1395i-3(g)(2)(B)(i) of this title or subsection (g)(2)(B)(i) of this section; or

(c) has been assessed a civil money penalty described in section 1395i-3(h)(2)(B)(ii) of this title or subsection (h)(2)(A)(ii) of this section of not less than $5,000, or has been subject to a remedy described in subsection (h)(1)(B)(i) of this section, clauses [3] (i), (iii), or (iv) of subsection (h)(2)(A) of this section, clauses (FOOTNOTE 3) (i) or (iii) of section 1395i-3(h)(2)(B) of this title, or section 1395i-3(h)(4) of this title, or

(II) offered by or in a nursing facility unless the State makes the determination, upon an individual's completion of the program, that the individual is competent to provide nursing and nursing-related services in nursing facilities. A State may not delegate (through subcontract or otherwise) its responsibility under clause (iii)(II) to the nursing facility.

(C) Waiver authorized

Clause (iii)(I) of subparagraph (B) shall not apply to a program offered in (but not by) a nursing facility (or skilled nursing facility for purposes of subchapter XVIII of this chapter) in a State if the State—

(i) determines that there is no other such program offered within a reasonable distance of the facility,

(ii) assures, through an oversight effort, that an adequate environment exists for operating the program in the facility, and

(iii) provides notice of such determination and assurances to the State long-term care ombudsman.

(3) Federal guidelines for State appeals process for transfers and discharges

For purposes of subsections (c)(2)(B)(iii) and (e)(3) of this section, by not later than October 1, 1988, the Secretary shall establish guidelines for minimum standards which State appeals processes under subsection (e)(3) of this section must meet to provide a fair mechanism for hearing appeals on transfers and discharges of residents from nursing facilities.

(4) Secretarial standards qualification of administrators

For purposes of subsections (d)(1)(C) and (e)(4) of this section, the Secretary shall develop, by not later than March 1, 1988, standards to be applied in assuring the qualifications of administrators of nursing facilities.

(5) Criteria for administration

The Secretary shall establish criteria for assessing a nursing facility's compliance with the requirement of subsection (d)(1) of this section with respect to—

(A) its governing body and management,

(B) agreements with hospitals regarding transfers of residents to and from the hospitals and to and from other nursing facilities,

(C) disaster preparedness,

(D) direction of medical care by a physician,

(E) laboratory and radiological services,

(F) clinical records, and

(G) resident and advocate participation.

(6) Specification of resident assessment data set and instruments

The Secretary shall—

(A) not later than January 1, 1989, specify a minimum data set of core elements and common definitions for use by nursing facilities in conducting the assessments required under subsection (b)(3) of this section, and establish guidelines for utilization of the data set; and

(B) by not later than April 1, 1990, designate one or more instruments which are consistent with the specification made under subparagraph (A) and which a State may specify under subsection (e)(5)(A) of this section for use by nursing facilities in complying with the requirements of subsection (b)(3)(A)(iii) of this section.

(7) List of items and services furnished in nursing facilities not chargeable to the personal funds of a resident

(A) Regulations required

Pursuant to the requirement of section 21(b) of the Medicare-Medicaid Anti-Fraud and Abuse Amendments of 1977, the Secretary shall issue regulations, on or before the first day of the seventh month to begin after December 22, 1987, that define those costs which may be charged to the personal funds of residents in nursing facilities who are individuals receiving medical assistance with respect to nursing facility services under this subchapter and those costs which are to be included in the payment amount under this subchapter for nursing facility services.

(B) Rule if failure to publish regulations

If the Secretary does not issue the r gulations under subparagraph (A) on or before the date required in that subparagraph, in the case of a resident of a nursing facility who is eligible to receive benefits for nursing facility services under this subchapter, for purposes of section 1396a(a)(28)(B) of this title, the Secretary shall be deemed to have promulgated regulations under this paragraph which provide that the costs which may not be charged to the personal funds of such resident (and for which payment is considered to be made under this subchapter) include, at a minimum, the costs for routine personal hygiene items and services furnished by the facility.

(8) Federal minimum criteria and monitoring for preadmission screening and resident review

(A) Minimum criteria

The Secretary shall develop, by not later than October 1, 1988, minimum criteria for States to use in making determinations under subsections (b)(3)(F) and (e)(7)(B) of this section and in permitting individuals adversely affected to appeal such determinations, and shall notify the States of such criteria.

(B) Monitoring compliance

The Secretary shall review, in a sufficient number of cases to allow reasonable inferences, each State's compliance with the requirements of subsection (e)(7)(C)(ii) of this section (relating to discharge and placement for active treatment of certain residents).

(9) Criteria for monitoring State waivers

The Secretary shall develop, by not later than October 1, 1988, criteria and procedures for monitoring State performances in granting waivers pursuant to subsection (b)(4)(C)(ii) of this section.

(g) Survey and certification process

(1) State and Federal responsibility

(A) In general

Under each State plan under this subchapter, the State shall be responsible for certifying, in accordance with surveys conducted under paragraph (2), the compliance of nursing facilities (other than facilities of the State) with the requirements of subsections (b), (c), and (d) of this section. The Secretary shall be responsible for certifying, in accordance with surveys conducted under paragraph (2), the compliance of State nursing facilities with the requirements of such subsections.

(B) Educational program

Each State shall conduct periodic educational programs for the staff and residents (and their representatives) of nursing facilities in order to present current regulations, procedures, and policies under this section.

(C) Investigation of allegations of resident neglect and abuse and misappropriation of resident property

The State shall provide, through the agency responsible for surveys and certification of nursing facilities under this subsection, for a process for the receipt and timely review and investigation of allegations of neglect and abuse and misappropriation of resident property by a nurse aide of a resident in a nursing facility or by another individual used by the facility in providing services to such a resident. The State shall, after notice to the individual involved and a reasonable opportunity for a hearing for the individual to rebut allegations, make a finding as to the accuracy of the allegations. If the State finds that a nurse aide has neglected or abused a resident or misappropriated resident property in a facility, the State shall notify the nurse aide and the registry of such finding. If the State finds that any other individual used by the facility has neglected or abused a resident or misappropriated resident property in a facility, the State shall notify the appropriate licensure authority. A State shall not make a finding that an individual has neglected a resident if the individual demonstrates that such neglect was caused by factors beyond the control of the individual.

(D) Removal of name from nurse aide registry

(i) In general

In the case of a finding of neglect under subparagraph (C), the State shall establish a procedure to permit a nurse aide to petition the State to have his or her name removed from the registry upon a determination by the State that—

(I) the employment and personal history of the nurse aide does not reflect a pattern of abusive behavior or neglect; and

(II) the neglect involved in the original finding was a singular occurrence.

(ii) Timing of determination

In no case shall a determination on a petition submitted under clause (i) be made prior to the expiration of the 1-year period beginning on the date on which the name of the petitioner was added to the registry under subparagraph (C).

(E) Construction

The failure of the Secretary to issue regulations to carry out this subsection shall not relieve a State of its responsibility under this subsection.

(2) Surveys

(A) Annual standard survey

(i) In general

Each nursing facility shall be subject to a standard survey, to be conducted without any prior notice to the facility. Any individual who notifies (or causes to be notified) a nursing facility of the time or date on which such a survey is scheduled to be conducted is subject to a civil money penalty of not to exceed $2,000. The provisions of section 1320a-7a of this title (other than subsections (a) and (b)) shall apply to a civil money penalty under the previous sentence in the same manner as such provisions apply to a penalty or proceeding under section 1320a-7a(a) of this title. The Secretary shall review each State's procedures for scheduling and conduct of standard surveys to assure that the State has taken all reasonable steps to avoid giving notice of such a survey through the scheduling procedures and the conduct of the surveys themselves.

(ii) Contents

Each standard survey shall include, for a case-mix stratified sample of residents—

(I) a survey of the quality of care furnished, as measured by indicators of medical, nursing, and rehabilitative care, dietary and nutrition services, activities and social participation, and sanitation, infection control, and the physical environment,

(II) written plans of care provided under subsection (b)(2) of this section and an audit of the residents' assessments under subsection (b)(3) of this section to determine the accuracy of such assessments and the adequacy of such plans of care, and

(III) a review of compliance with residents' rights under subsection (c) of this section.

(iii) Frequency

(I) In general

Each nursing facility shall be subject to a standard survey not later than 15 months after the date of the previous standard survey conducted under this subparagraph. The statewide average interval between standard surveys of a nursing facility shall not exceed 12 months.

(II) Special surveys

If not otherwise conducted under subclause (I), a standard survey (or an abbreviated standard survey) may be conducted within 2 months of any change of ownership, administration, management of a nursing facility, or director of nursing in order to determine whether the change has resulted in any decline in the quality of care furnished in the facility.

(B) Extended surveys

(i) In general

Each nursing facility which is found, under a standard survey, to have provided substandard quality of care shall be subject to an extended survey. Any other facility may, at the Secretary's or State's discretion, be subject to such an extended survey (or a partial extended survey).

(ii) Timing

The extended survey shall be conducted immediately after the standard survey (or, if not practicable, not later than 2 weeks after the date of completion of the standard survey).

(iii) Contents

In such an extended survey, the survey team shall review and identify the policies and procedures which produced such substandard quality of care and shall determine whether the facility has complied with all the requirements described in subsections (b), (c), and (d) of this section. Such review shall include an expansion of the size of the sample of residents' assessments reviewed and a review of the staffing, of in-service training, and, if appropriate, of contracts with consultants.

(iv) Construction

Nothing in this paragraph shall be construed as requiring an extended or partial extended survey as a prerequisite to imposing a sanction against a facility under subsection (h) of this section on the basis of findings in a standard survey.

(C) Survey protocol

Standard and extended surveys shall be conducted—

(i) based upon a protocol which the Secretary has developed, tested, and validated by not later than January 1, 1990, and

(ii) by individuals, of a survey team, who meet such minimum qualifications as the Secretary establishes by not later than such date.

The failure of the Secretary to develop, test, or validate such protocols or to establish such minimum qualifications shall not relieve any State of its responsibility (or the Secretary of the Secretary's responsibility) to conduct surveys under this subsection.

(D) Consistency of surveys

Each State shall implement programs to measure and reduce inconsistency in the application of survey results among surveyors.

(E) Survey teams

(i) In general

Surveys under this subsection shall be conducted by a multidisciplinary team of professionals (including a registered professional nurse).

(ii) Prohibition of conflicts of interest

A State may not use as a member of a survey team under this subsection an individual who is serving (or has served within the previous 2 years) as a member of the staff of, or as a consultant to, the facility surveyed respecting compliance with the requirements of subsections (b), (c), and (d) of this section, or who has a personal or familial financial interest in the facility being surveyed.

(iii) Training

The Secretary shall provide for the comprehensive training of State and Federal surveyors in the conduct of standard and extended surveys under this subsection, including the auditing of resident assessments and plans of care. No individual shall serve as a member of a survey team unless the individual has successfully completed a training and testing program in survey and certification techniques that has been approved by the Secretary.

(3) Validation surveys

(A) In general

The Secretary shall conduct onsite surveys of a representative sample of nursing facilities in each State, within 2 months of the date of surveys conducted under paragraph (2) by the State, in a sufficient number to allow inferences about the adequacies of each State's surveys conducted under paragraph (2). In conducting such surveys, the Secretary shall use the same survey protocols as the State is required to use under paragraph (2). If the State has determined that an individual nursing facility meets the requirements of subsections (b), (c), and (d) of this section, but the Secretary determines that the facility does not meet such requirements, the Secretary's determination as to the facility's noncompliance with such requirements is binding and supersedes that of the State survey.

(B) Scope

With respect to each State, the Secretary shall conduct surveys under subparagraph (A) each year with respect to at least 5 percent of the number of nursing facilities surveyed by the State in the year, but in no case less than 5 nursing facilities in the State.

(C) Reduction in administrative costs for substandard performance

If the Secretary finds, on the basis of such surveys, that a State has failed to perform surveys as required under paragraph (2) or that a State's survey and certification performance otherwise is not adequate, the Secretary may provide for the training of survey teams in the State and shall provide for a reduction of the payment otherwise made to the State under section 1396b(a)(2)(D) of this title with respect to a quarter equal to 33 percent multiplied by a fraction, the denominator of which is equal to the total number of residents in nursing facilities surveyed by the Secretary that quarter and the numerator of which is equal to the total number of residents in nursing facilities which were found pursuant to such surveys to be not in compliance with any of the requirements of subsections (b), (c), and (d) of this section. A State that is dissatisfied with the Secretary's findings under this subparagraph may obtain reconsideration and review of the findings under section 1316 of this title in the same manner as a State may seek reconsideration and review under that section of the Secretary's determination under section 1316(a)(1) of this title.

(D) Special surveys of compliance

Where the Secretary has reason to question the compliance of a nursing facility with any of the requirements of subsections (b), (c), and (d) of this section, the Secretary may conduct a survey of the facility and, on the basis of that survey, make independent and binding determinations concerning the extent to which the nursing facility meets such requirements.

(4) Investigation of complaints and monitoring nursing facility compliance

Each State shall maintain procedures and adequate staff to—

(A) investigate complaints of violations of requirements by nursing facilities, and

(B) monitor, on-site, on a regular, as needed basis, a nursing facility's compliance with the requirements of subsections (b), (c), and (d) of this section, if—

(i) the facility has been found not to be in compliance with such requirements and is in the process of correcting deficiencies to achieve such compliance;

(ii) the facility was previously found not to be in compliance with such requirements, has corrected deficiencies to achieve such compliance, and verification of continued compliance is indicated; or

(iii) the State has reason to question the compliance of the facility with such requirements.

A State may maintain and utilize a specialized team (including an attorney, an auditor, and appropriate health care professionals) for the purpose of identifying, surveying, gathering and preserving evidence, and carrying out appropriate enforcement actions against substandard nursing facilities.

(5) Disclosure of results of inspections and activities

(A) Public information

Each State, and the Secretary, shall make available to the public—

> (i) information respecting all surveys and certifications made respecting nursing facilities, including statements of deficiencies, within 14 calendar days after such information is made available to those facilities, and approved plans of correction,

> (ii) copies of cost reports of such facilities filed under this subchapter or under subchapter XVIII of this chapter,

> (iii) copies of statements of ownership under section 1320a-3 of this title, and

> (iv) information disclosed under section 1320a-5 of this title.

(B) Notice to ombudsman

Each State shall notify the State long-term care ombudsman (established under title III or VII of the Older Americans Act of 1965 (42 U.S.C. 3021 et seq., 3058 et seq.) in accordance with section 712 of the Act (42 U.S.C. 3058g)) of the State's findings of noncompliance with any of the requirements of subsections (b), (c), and (d) of this section, or of any adverse action taken against a nursing facility under paragraphs [4] (1), (2), or (3) of subsection (h) of this section, with respect to a nursing facility in the State.

(C) Notice to physicians and nursing facility administrator licensing board

If a State finds that a nursing facility has provided substandard quality of care, the State shall notify—

> (i) the attending physician of each resident with respect to which such finding is made, and

> (ii) any State board responsible for the licensing of the nursing facility administrator of the facility.

(D) Access to fraud control units

Each State shall provide its State medicaid fraud and abuse control unit (established under section 1396b(q) of this title) with access to all information of the State agency responsible for surveys and certifications under this subsection.

(h) Enforcement process

(1) In general

If a State finds, on the basis of a standard, extended, or partial extended survey under subsection (g)(2) of this section or otherwise, that a nursing facility no longer meets a requirement of subsection (b), (c), or (d) of this section, and further finds that the facility's deficiencies—

(A) immediately jeopardize the health or safety of its residents, the State shall take immediate action to remove the jeopardy and correct the deficiencies through the remedy specified in paragraph (2)(A)(iii), or terminate the facility's participation under the State plan and may provide, in addition, for one or more of the other remedies described in paragraph (2); or

(B) do not immediately jeopardize the health or safety of its residents, the State may—

(i) terminate the facility's participation under the State plan,

(ii) provide for one or more of the remedies described in paragraph (2), or

(iii) do both.

Nothing in this paragraph shall be construed as restricting the remedies available to a State to remedy a nursing facility's deficiencies. If a State finds that a nursing facility meets the requirements of subsections (b), (c), and (d) of this section, but, as of a previous period, did not meet such requirements, the State may provide for a civil money penalty under paragraph (2)(A)(ii) for the days in which it finds that the facility was not in compliance with such requirements.

(2) Specified remedies

(A) Listing

Except as provided in subparagraph (B)(ii), each State shall establish by law (whether statute or regulation) at least the following remedies:

(i) Denial of payment under the State plan with respect to any individual admitted to the nursing facility involved after such notice to the public and to the facility as may be provided for by the State.

(ii) A civil money penalty assessed and collected, with interest, for each day in which the facility is or was out of compliance with a requirement of subsection (b), (c), or (d) of this section. Funds collected by a State as a result of imposition of such a penalty (or as a result of the imposition by the State of a civil money penalty for activities described in subsections (b)(3)(B)(ii)(I), (b)(3)(B)(ii)(II), or (g)(2)(A)(i) of this section) shall be applied to the protection of the health or property of residents of nursing facilities that the State or the Secretary finds deficient, including payment for the costs of relocation of residents to other facilities, maintenance of operation of a facility pending correction of deficiencies or closure, and reimbursement of residents for personal funds lost.

(iii) The appointment of temporary management to oversee the operation of the facility and to assure the health and safety of the facility's residents, where there is a need for temporary management while—

(I) there is an orderly closure of the facility, or

(II) improvements are made in order to bring the facility into compliance with all the requirements of subsections (b), (c), and (d) of this section. The temporary management under this clause shall not be terminated under subclause (II) until the State has determined that the facility has the management capability to ensure continued compliance with all the requirements of subsections (b), (c), and (d) of this section.

(iv) The authority, in the case of an emergency, to close the facility, to transfer residents in that facility to other facilities, or both.

The State also shall specify criteria, as to when and how each of such remedies is to be applied, the amounts of any fines, and the severity of each of these remedies, to be used in the imposition of such remedies. Such criteria shall be designed so as to minimize the time between the identification of violations and final imposition of the remedies and shall provide for the imposition of incrementally more severe fines for repeated or uncorrected deficiencies. In addition, the State may provide for other specified remedies, such as directed plans of correction.

(B) Deadline and guidance

(i) Except as provided in clause (ii), as a condition for approval of a State plan for calendar quarters beginning on or after October 1, 1989, each State shall establish the remedies described in clauses (i) through (iv) of subparagraph (A) by not later than October 1, 1989. The Secretary shall provide, through regulations by not later than October 1, 1988, guidance to States in establishing such remedies; but the failure of the Secretary to provide such guidance shall not relieve a State of the responsibility for establishing such remedies.

(ii) A State may establish alternative remedies (other than termination of participation) other than those described in clauses (i) through (iv) of subparagraph (A), if the State demonstrates to the Secretary's satisfaction that the alternative remedies are as effective in deterring noncompliance and correcting deficiencies as those described in subparagraph (A).

(C) Assuring prompt compliance

If a nursing facility has not complied with any of the requirements of subsections (b), (c), and (d) of this section, within 3 months after the date the facility is found to be out of compliance with such requirements, the State shall impose the remedy described in subparagraph (A)(i) for all individuals who are admitted to the facility after such date.

(D) Repeated noncompliance

In the case of a nursing facility which, on 3 consecutive standard surveys conducted under subsection (g)(2) of this section, has been found to have provided substandard quality of care, the State shall (regardless of what other remedies are provided)—

(i) impose the remedy described in subparagraph (A)(i), and

(ii) monitor the facility under subsection (g)(4)(B) of this section, until the facility has demonstrated, to the satisfaction of the State, that it is in compliance with the requirements of subsections (b), (c), and (d) of this section, and that it will remain in compliance with such requirements.

(E) Funding

The reasonable expenditures of a State to provide for temporary management and other expenses associated with implementing the remedies described in clauses (iii) and (iv) of subparagraph (A) shall be considered, for purposes of section 1396b(a)(7) of this title, to be necessary for the proper and efficient administration of the State plan.

(F) Incentives for high quality care

In addition to the remedies specified in this paragraph, a State may establish a program to reward, through public recognition, incentive payments, or both, nursing facilities that provide the highest quality care to residents who are entitled to medical assistance under this subchapter. For purposes of section 1396b(a)(7) of this title, proper expenses incurred by a State in carrying out such a program shall be considered to be expenses necessary for the proper and efficient administration of the State plan under this subchapter.

(3) Secretarial authority

(A) For State nursing facilities

With respect to a State nursing facility, the Secretary shall have the authority and duties of a State under this subsection, including the authority to impose remedies described in clauses (i), (ii), and (iii) of paragraph (2)(A).

(B) Other nursing facilities

With respect to any other nursing facility in a State, if the Secretary finds that a nursing facility no longer meets a requirement of subsection (b), (c), (d), or (e) of this section, and further finds that the facility's deficiencies—

(i) immediately jeopardize the health or safety of its residents, the Secretary shall take immediate action to remove the jeopardy and correct the deficiencies through the remedy specified in subparagraph (C)(iii), or terminate the facility's participation under the State plan and may provide, in addition, for one or more of the other remedies described in subparagraph (C); or

(ii) do not immediately jeopardize the health or safety of its residents, the Secretary may impose any of the remedies described in subparagraph (C).

Nothing in this subparagraph shall be construed as restricting the remedies available to the Secretary to remedy a nursing facility's deficiencies. If the Secretary finds that a nursing facility meets such requirements but, as of a previous period, did not meet such requirements, the Secretary may provide for a civil money penalty under subparagraph (C)(ii) for the days on which he finds that the facility was not in compliance with such requirements.

(C) Specified remedies

The Secretary may take the following actions with respect to a finding that a facility has not met an applicable requirement:

(i) Denial of payment

The Secretary may deny any further payments to the State for medical assistance furnished by the facility to all individuals in the facility or to individuals admitted to the facility after the effective date of the finding.

(ii) Authority with respect to civil money penalties

The Secretary may impose a civil money penalty in an amount not to exceed $10,000 for each day of noncompliance. The provisions of section 1320a-7a of this title (other than subsections (a) and (b)) shall apply to a civil money penalty under the previous sentence in the same manner as such provisions apply to a penalty or proceeding under section 1320a-7a(a) of this title.

(iii) Appointment of temporary management

In consultation with the State, the Secretary may appoint temporary management to oversee the operation of the facility and to assure the health and safety of the facility's residents, where there is a need for temporary management while—

(I) there is an orderly closure of the facility, or

(II) improvements are made in order to bring the facility into compliance with all the requirements of subsections (b), (c), and (d) of this section. The temporary management under this clause shall not be terminated under subclause (II) until the Secretary has determined that the facility has the management capability to ensure continued compliance with all the requirements of subsections (b), (c), and (d) of this section.

The Secretary shall specify criteria, as to when and how each of such remedies is to be applied, the amounts of any fines, and the severity of each of these remedies, to be used in the imposition of such remedies. Such criteria shall be designed so as to minimize the time between the identification of violations and final imposition of the remedies and shall provide for the imposition of incrementally more severe fines for repeated or uncorrected deficiencies. In addition, the Secretary may provide for other specified remedies, such as directed plans of correction.

(D) Continuation of payments pending remediation

The Secretary may continue payments, over a period of not longer than 6 months after the effective date of the findings, under this subchapter with respect to a nursing facility not in compliance with a requirement of subsection (b), (c), or (d) of this section, if—

(i) the State survey agency finds that it is more appropriate to take alternative action to assure compliance of the facility with the requirements than to terminate the certification of the facility, and

(ii) the State has submitted a plan and timetable for corrective action to the Secretary for approval and the Secretary approves the plan of corrective action.

The Secretary shall establish guidelines for approval of corrective actions requested by States under this subparagraph.

(4) Effective period of denial of payment

A finding to deny payment under this subsection shall terminate when the State or Secretary (or both, as the case may be) finds that the facility is in substantial compliance with all the requirements of subsections (b), (c), and (d) of this section.

(5) Immediate termination of participation for facility where State or Secretary finds noncompliance and immediate jeopardy

If either the State or the Secretary finds that a nursing facility has not met a requirement of subsection (b), (c), or (d) of this section, and finds that the failure immediately jeopardizes the health or safety of its residents, the State or the Secretary, respectively [5] shall notify the other of such finding, and the State or the Secretary, respectively, shall take immediate action to remove the jeopardy and correct the deficiencies through the remedy specified in paragraph (2)(A)(iii) or (3)(C)(iii), or terminate the facility's participation under the State plan. If the facility's participation in the State plan is terminated by either the State or the Secretary, the State shall provide for the safe and orderly transfer of the residents eligible under the State plan consistent with the requirements of subsection (c)(2) of this section.

(6) Special rules where State and Secretary do not agree on finding of noncompliance

(A) State finding of noncompliance and no Secretarial finding of noncompliance

If the Secretary finds that a nursing facility has met all the requirements of subsections (b), (c), and (d) of this section, but a State finds that the facility has not met such requirements and the failure does not immediately jeopardize the health or safety of its residents, the State's findings shall control and the remedies imposed by the State shall be applied.

(B) Secretarial finding of noncompliance and no State finding of noncompliance

If the Secretary finds that a nursing facility has not met all the requirements of subsections (b), (c), and (d) of this section, and that the failure does not immediately jeopardize the health or safety of its residents, but the State has not made such a finding, the Secretary—

(i) may impose any remedies specified in paragraph (3)(C) with respect to the facility, and

(ii) shall (pending any termination by the Secretary) permit continuation of payments in accordance with paragraph (3)(D).

(7) Special rules for timing of termination of participation where remedies overlap

If both the Secretary and the State find that a nursing facility has not met all the requirements of subsections (b), (c), and (d) of this section, and neither finds that the failure immediately jeopardizes the health or safety of its residents—

(A) (i) if both find that the facility's participation under the State plan should be terminated, the State's timing of any termination shall control so long as the termination date does not occur later than 6 months after the date of the finding to terminate;

(ii) if the Secretary, but not the State, finds that the facility's participation under the State plan should be terminated, the Secretary shall (pending any termination by the Secretary) permit continuation of payments in accordance with paragraph (3)(D); or

(iii) if the State, but not the Secretary, finds that the facility's participation under the State plan should be terminated, the State's decision to terminate, and timing of such termination, shall control; and

(B)(i) if the Secretary or the State, but not both, establishes one or more remedies which are additional or alternative to the remedy of terminating the facility's participation under the State plan, such additional or alternative remedies shall also be applied, or

(ii) if both the Secretary and the State establish one or more remedies which are additional or alternative to the remedy of terminating the facility's participation under the State plan, only the additional or alternative remedies of the Secretary shall apply.

(8) Construction

The remedies provided under this subsection are in addition to those otherwise available under State or Federal law and shall not be construed as limiting such other remedies, including any remedy available to an individual at common law. The remedies described in clauses (i), (iii), and (iv) of paragraph (2)(A) may be imposed during the pendency of any hearing. The provisions of this subsection shall apply to a nursing facility (or portion thereof) notwithstanding that the facility (or portion thereof) also is a skilled nursing facility for purposes of subchapter XVIII of this chapter.

(9) Sharing of information

Notwithstanding any other provision of law, all information concerning nursing facilities required by this section to be filed with the Secretary or a State agency shall be made available by such facilities to Federal or State employees for purposes consistent with the effective administration of programs established under this subchapter and subchapter XVIII of this chapter, including investigations by State medicaid fraud control units.

(i) Construction

Where requirements or obligations under this section are identical to those provided under section 1395i-3 of this title, the fulfillment of those requirements or obligations under section 1395i-3 of this title shall be considered to be the fulfillment of the corresponding requirements or obligations under this section.

APPENDIX 12:
TITLE VII OF THE OLDER AMERICANS ACT: VULNERABLE ELDER RIGHTS PROTECTION

PART A—SECTION 30581. PREVENTION OF ELDER ABUSE, NEGLECT, AND EXPLOITATION

(a) Establishment

In order to be eligible to receive an allotment under section 3058b of this title from funds appropriated under section 3058a(b) of this title, a State agency shall, in accordance with this section, and in consultation with area agencies on aging, develop and enhance programs for the prevention of elder abuse, neglect, and exploitation.

(b) Use of allotments

The State agency shall use an allotment made under subsection (a) of this section to carry out, through the programs described in subsection (a) of this section, activities to develop, strengthen, and carry out programs for the prevention and treatment of elder abuse, neglect, and exploitation, including—

(1) providing for public education and outreach to identify and prevent elder abuse, neglect, and exploitation;

(2) ensuring the coordination of services provided by area agencies on aging with services instituted under the State adult protection service program;

(3) promoting the development of information and data systems, including elder abuse reporting systems, to quantify the extent of elder abuse, neglect, and exploitation in the State;

(4) conducting analyses of State information concerning elder abuse, neglect, and exploitation and identifying unmet service, enforcement, or intervention needs;

(5) conducting training for individuals, professionals, and paraprofessionals, in relevant fields on the identification, prevention, and treatment of elder abuse, neglect, and exploitation, with particular focus on prevention and enhancement of self-determination and autonomy;

(6) providing technical assistance to programs that provide or have the potential to provide services for victims of elder abuse, neglect, and exploitation and for family members of the victims;

(7) conducting special and on-going training, for individuals involved in serving victims of elder abuse, neglect, and exploitation, on the topics of self-determination, individual rights, State and Federal requirements concerning confidentiality, and other topics determined by a State agency to be appropriate; and

(8) promoting the development of an elder abuse, neglect, and exploitation system—

(A) that includes a State elder abuse, neglect, and exploitation law that includes provisions for immunity, for persons reporting instances of elder abuse, neglect, and exploitation, from prosecution arising out of such reporting, under any State or local law;

(B) under which a State agency—

(i) on receipt of a report of known or suspected instances of elder abuse, neglect, or exploitation, shall promptly initiate an investigation to substantiate the accuracy of the report; and

(ii) on a finding of elder abuse, neglect, or exploitation, shall take steps, including appropriate referral, to protect the health and welfare of the abused, neglected, or exploited older individual;

(C) that includes, throughout the State, in connection with the enforcement of elder abuse, neglect, and exploitation laws and with the reporting of suspected instances of elder abuse, neglect, and exploitation—

(i) such administrative procedures;

(ii) such personnel trained in the special problems of elder abuse, neglect, and exploitation prevention and treatment;

(iii) such training procedures;

(iv) such institutional and other facilities (public and private); and

(v) such related multidisciplinary programs and services, as may be necessary or appropriate to ensure that the State will deal effectively with elder abuse, neglect, and exploitation cases in the State;

(D) that preserves the confidentiality of records in order to protect the rights of older individuals;

(E) that provides for the cooperation of law enforcement officials, courts of competent jurisdiction, and State agencies providing human services with respect to special problems of elder abuse, neglect, and exploitation;

F) that enables an older individual to participate in decisions re - garding the welfare of the older individual, and makes the least restrictive alternatives available to an older individual who is abused, neglected, or exploited; and

(G) that includes a State clearinghouse for dissemination of information to the general public with respect to—

(i) the problems of elder abuse, neglect, and exploitation;

(ii) the facilities described in subparagraph (C)(iv); and

(iii) prevention and treatment methods available to combat instances of elder abuse, neglect, and exploitation.

(c) Approach

In developing and enhancing programs under subsection (a) of this section, the State agency shall use a comprehensive approach, in consultation with area agencies on aging, to identify and assist older individuals who are subject to abuse, neglect, and exploitation, including older individuals who live in State licensed facilities, unlicensed facilities, or domestic or community-based settings.

(d) Coordination

In developing and enhancing programs under subsection (a) of this section, the State agency shall coordinate the programs with other State and local programs and services for the protection of vulnerable adults, particularly vulnerable older individuals, including programs and services such as—

(1) area agency on aging programs;

(2) adult protective service programs;

(3) the State Long-Term Care Ombudsman program established in subpart II of this part;

(4) protection and advocacy programs;

(5) facility and long-term care provider licensure and certification programs;

(6) medicaid fraud and abuse services, including services provided by a State medicaid fraud control unit, as defined in section 1396b(q) of this title;

(7) victim assistance programs; and

(8) consumer protection and law enforcement programs, as well as other State and local programs that identify and assist vulnerable older individuals.

(e) Requirements

In developing and enhancing programs under subsection (a) of this section, the State agency shall—

(1) not permit involuntary or coerced participation in such programs by alleged victims, abusers, or members of their households;

(2) require that all information gathered in the course of receiving a report described in subsection (b)(8)(B)(i) of this section, and making a referral described in subsection (b)(8)(B)(ii) of this section, shall remain confidential except—

(A) if all parties to such complaint or report consent in writing to the release of such information;

(B) if the release of such information is to a law enforcement agency, public protective service agency, licensing or certification agency, ombudsman program, or protection or advocacy system; or

(C) upon court order; and

(3) make all reasonable efforts to resolve any conflicts with other public agencies with respect to confidentiality of the information described in paragraph (2) by entering into memoranda of understanding that narrowly limit disclosure of information, consistent with the requirement described in paragraph (2).

(f) Designation

The State agency may designate a State entity to carry out the programs and activities described in this subpart.

APPENDIX 13:
STATE STATUTES CONCERNING ELDER ABUSE

STATE	ADULT PROTECTIVE SERVICES	INSTITUTIONAL ABUSE	LONG-TERM CARE OMBUDSMAN PROGRAM
Alabama	Ala. Code §38-9-1 et seq.	N/A	Ala. Code §22-5A-1 et seq.
Alaska	Alaska Stat. §47.24.010 et seq.	N/A	Alaska Stat. §44.21.231 et seq.
Arizona	Ariz. Rev. Stat. Ann. §46-451 et seq.	N/A	Ariz. Rev. Stat. Ann. §46-452.01 & .02
Arkansas	Ark. Code Ann. §5-28-101 et seq.	N/A	Ark. Code Ann. §20-10-601 et seq.
California	Cal. Welf. & Inst. Code §15750 et seq.	N/A	Cal. Welf. & Inst. Code §9700 et seq.
Colorado	Colo. Rev. Stat. Ann. §26-3.1-101 et seq.	N/A	Colo. Rev. Stat. Ann. §26-11.5-101 et seq.
Connecticut	Conn. Gen. Stat. Ann. §17b-450 et seq.	N/A	Conn. Gen. Stat. Ann. §17b-400 et seq.
Delaware	Del. Code Ann. tit. 31, §3901 et seq.	Del. Code Ann. tit. 16, §1131 et seq.	Del. Code Ann. tit. 16, §1150 et seq.
District of Columbia	D.C. Code Ann. §6-2501 et seq.	N/A	D.C. Code Ann. §6-3501
Florida	Fla. Stat. Ann. §415.101 et seq.	N/A	Fla. Stat. Ann. §400.0060 et seq.

STATE	ADULT PROTECTIVE SERVICES	INSTITUTIONAL ABUSE	LONG-TERM CARE OMBUDSMAN PROGRAM
Georgia	Ga. Code Ann. §30-5-1 et seq.	Ga. Code Ann. §31-8-80 et seq.	Ga. Code Ann. §31-8-51 et seq.
Hawaii	Haw. Rev. Stat. §346-221 et seq.	N/A	Haw. Rev. Stat. §349-12 et seq.
Idaho	Idaho Code §39-5301 et seq.	N/A	Idaho Code §67-5009 et seq.
Illinois	320 Ill. Comp. Stat. 20/1 et seq.	210 Ill. Comp. Stat. 30/1 et seq.	20 Ill. Comp. Stat. 105/4.04
Indiana	Ind. Code Ann. §12-10-3-1 et seq.	N/A	Ind. Code Ann. §12-10-13 et seq.
Iowa	Iowa Code Ann. §235B.1 et seq.	N/A	Iowa Code Ann. §231.41 et seq.
Kansas	Kan. Stat. Ann. §39-1430 et seq.	Kan. Stat. Ann. §39-1401 et seq.	Kan. Stat. Ann. §75-5916 et seq.
Kentucky	Ky. Rev. Stat. Ann. §209.005 et seq.	N/A	Ky. Rev. Stat. Ann. §216.541& 905
Louisiana	La. Rev. Stat. Ann. §14:403.2 et seq.	N/A	La. Rev. Stat. Ann. §40:2010.1 et seq.
Maine	Me. Rev. Stat. Ann. tit. 22, §3470 et seq.	N/A	Me. Rev. Stat. Ann. tit. 22, §5107-A et seq.
Maryland	Md. Code Ann., Fam. Law §14-101 et seq.	Md. Code Ann., Health §19-347	Md. Code Ann., Art. 70B §5
Massachusetts	Mass. Gen. Laws Ann. ch. 19A, §14 et seq.	Mass. Gen. Laws Ann. ch. 111, §72F et seq.	Mass. Gen. Laws Ann. ch. 19A, §27 et seq.
Michigan	Mich. Comp. Laws Ann. §400.11 et seq.	Mich. Comp. Laws Ann. §400.11f	Mich. Comp. Laws Ann. §400.586g et seq.
Minnesota	Minn. Stat. Ann. §626.557 et seq.	N/A	Minn. Stat. Ann. §256.974 et seq.
Mississippi	Miss. Code Ann. §43-47-1 et seq.	Miss. Code Ann. §43-47-37	Miss. Code Ann. §43-7-51 et seq.
Missouri	Mo. Ann. Stat. §660.250 et seq. & §660.300 et seq.	Mo. Ann. Stat. §198.070	Mo. Ann. Stat. §660.600 et seq.

STATE	ADULT PROTECTIVE SERVICES	INSTITUTIONAL ABUSE	LONG-TERM CARE OMBUDSMAN PROGRAM
Montana	Mont. Code Ann. §52-3-801 et seq.	N/A	Mont. Code Ann. §52-3-601 et seq.
Nebraska	Neb. Rev. Stat. §28-348 et seq.	N/A	Neb. Rev. Stat. §81-2237 et seq.
Nevada	Nev. Rev. Stat. Ann. §200.5091 et seq.	N/A	Nev. Rev. Stat. Ann. §427A.125 et seq.
New Hampshire	N.H. Rev. Stat. Ann. §161-F:42 et seq.	N/A	N.H. Rev. Stat. Ann. §161-F:10 et seq.
New Jersey	N.J. Stat. Ann. §52:27D-406 et seq.	N.J. Stat. Ann. §52:27G-7.1	N.J. Stat. Ann. §52:27G-1 et seq.
New Mexico	N.M. Stat. Ann. §27-7-14 et seq.	N/A	N.M. Stat. Ann. §28-17-1 et seq.
New York	N.Y. Soc. Serv. Law, Art. 9B, §473 et seq.	N/A	N.Y. Exec. Law, Art. 19J, §544-a et seq.
North Carolina	N.C. Gen. Stat. §108A-99 et seq.	N/A	N.C. Gen. Stat. §143B-181.15 et seq.
North Dakota	N.D. Cent. Code §50-25.2 et seq.	N/A	N.D. Cent. Code §50-10.1-01 et seq.
Ohio	Ohio Rev. Code Ann. §5101.60 et seq.	N/A	Ohio Rev. Code Ann. §173.14 et seq.
Oklahoma	Okla. Stat. Ann. tit. 43A, §10-101 et seq.	N/A	Okla. Stat. Ann. tit. 63, §1-2211 et seq.
Oregon	Or. Rev. Stat. §124.050 et seq.	Or. Rev. Stat. §441.630 et seq.	Or. Rev. Stat. §441.100 et seq.
Pennsylvania	35 Pa. Cons. Stat. Ann. §10225.101 et seq.	N/A	71 Pa. Cons. Stat. Ann. §581-3 (24.2)
Rhode Island	R.I. Gen. Laws §42-66-4.1 et seq.	R.I. Gen. Laws §23-17.8-1 et seq.	R.I. Gen. Laws §42-66.7-1 et seq.
South Carolina	S.C. Code Ann. §43-35-5 et seq.	N/A	S.C. Code Ann. §43-38-10 et seq.
South Dakota	S.D. Codified Laws Ann. §22-46-1 et seq.	N/A	S.D. Codified Laws Ann. §28-1-45.6 et seq.

STATE	ADULT PROTECTIVE SERVICES	INSTITUTIONAL ABUSE	LONG-TERM CARE OMBUDSMAN PROGRAM
Tennessee	Tenn. Code Ann. §71-6-101 et seq.	N/A	Tenn. Code Ann. §71-2-111
Texas	Tex. Hum. Res. Code Ann. §48.001 et seq.	Tex. Health & Safety Code Ann. §242.121. et seq.	Tex. Hum. Res. Code Ann. §101.051 et seq.
Utah	Utah Code Ann. §62A-3-301 et seq.	N/A	Utah Code Ann. §62A-3-201 et seq.

APPENDIX 14:
DIRECTORY OF NATIONAL LEGAL
SERVICES FOR THE ELDERLY

NAME	ADDRESS	TELEPHONE NUMBER
American Bar Association Commission on Legal Problems of the Elderly	1800 M Street N.W., Suite 200 Washington, DC 20036	202-331-2297
Center for Social Gerontology	117 No. 1st Street, Suite 204 Ann Arbor, MI 48104	313-665-1126
Legal Counsel for the Elderly	1909 K Street N.W. Washington, DC 20049	
Legal Services for the Elderly	132 W. 43rd Street, 3rd Floor New York, NY 10036	212-595-1340
Medicare Beneficiaries Defense Fund	1460 Broadway, 8th Floor New York, NY 10036	212-869-3850
National Academy of Elder Law Attorneys	1604 N. Country Club Road Tucson, AZ 85716	520-881-4005
National Caucus and Center on Black Aged	1424 K Street, NW, Suite 500 Washington, DC 20005	202-637-8400
National Health Law Program	2639 S. La Cienega Blvd. Los Angeles, CA 90034	213-204-6010
National Health Law Program	2025 M Street N.W. Washington, DC 20036	202-887-5310
National Senior Citizens Law Center	1052 W. 6th Street, 7th Floor Los Angeles, CA 90017	213-482-3550
National Senior Citizens Law Center	1101 14th Street N.W. Suite 400 Washington, DC 20005	202-887-5280

GLOSSARY

Accrue—To occur or come into existence.

Accreditation—A facility gains accreditation when it meets certain quality standards.

Act—Legislation passed by Congress.

Action at Law—A judicial proceeding whereby one party prosecutes another for a wrong done.

Actionable—Giving rise to a cause of action.

Actionable Negligence—The breach or nonperformance of a legal duty through neglect or carelessness, resulting in damage or injury to another.

Activities of Daily Living—Activities usually performed during the course of a normal day, e.g., bathing, dressing, eating, etc.

Actual Damages—Actual damages are those damages directly referable to the breach or tortious act, and which can be readily proven to have been sustained, and for which the injured party should be compensated as a matter of right.

Ad Damnum Clause—The clause in a complaint which sets forth the amount of damages demanded.

Adjudication—The determination of a controversy and pronouncement of judgment.

Admissible Evidence—Evidence which may be received by a trial court to assist the trier of fact, either the judge or jury, in deciding a dispute.

Admitting Physician—The doctor that admits a person to a hospital or other in-patient health facility.

Adversary—Opponent or litigant in a legal controversy or litigation.

Affirmative Defense—In a pleading, a matter constituting a defense.

Agency—The relationship between a principal and an agent who is employed by the principal, to perform certain acts dealing with third parties.

Agent—One who represents another known as the principal.

Allegation—Statement of the issue that the contributing party is prepared to prove.

Alzheimer's Disease—Disorder involving deterioration of mental functions resulting from changes in brain tissues.

Ambulatory Care—Health services that do not require in-patient hospital care.

Answer—In a civil proceeding, the principal pleading on the part of the defendant in response to the plaintiff's complaint.

Appearance—To come into court, personally or through an attorney, after being summoned.

Argument—A discourse set forth for the purpose of establishing one's position in a controversy.

Assault—A willful attempt or threat to harm another person which causes apprehension in that person.

Assessment—The gathering of information in order to evaluate a person's health and health-care needs.

Assumption of Risk—The legal doctrine that a plaintiff may not recover for an injury to which he assents.

Attorney In Fact—An attorney-in-fact is an agent or representative of another given authority to act in that person's name and place pursuant to a document called a "power of attorney."

Battery—The unlawful application of force to the person of another.

Bedsore—A pressure-induced skin ulceration.

Breach of Contract—The failure, without any legal excuse, to perform any promise which forms the whole or the part of a contract.

Breach of Duty—In a general sense, any violation or omission of a legal or moral duty.

Burden of Proof—The duty of a party to substantiate an allegation or issue to convince the trier of fact as to the truth of their claim.

Capacity—Capacity is the legal qualification concerning the ability of one to understand the nature and effects of one's acts.

Caption—The heading of a legal document which contains the name of the court, the index number assigned to the matter, and the names of the parties.

Cause of Action—The factual basis for bringing a lawsuit.

Child Abuse—Any form of cruelty to a child's physical, moral or mental well-being.

Child Protective Agency—A state agency responsible for the investigation of child abuse and neglect reports.

Circumstantial Evidence—Indirect evidence by which a principal fact may be inferred.

Coerce—To compel by pressure, threat, or force.

Compensatory Damages—Compensatory damages are those damages directly referable to a breach or tortious act, and which can be readily proven to have been sustained, and for which the injured party should be compensated as a matter of right.

Complaint—In a civil proceeding, the first pleading of the plaintiff setting out the facts on which the claim for relief is based.

Compromise and Settlement—An arrangement arrived at, either in court or out of court, for settling a dispute upon what appears to the parties to be equitable terms.

Conclusion of Fact—A conclusion reached by natural inference and based solely on the facts presented.

Conclusion of Law—A conclusion reached through the application of rules of law.

Conclusive Evidence—Evidence which is incontrovertible.

Contingency Fee—The fee charged by an attorney, which is dependent upon a successful outcome in the case, and is often agreed to be a percentage of the party's recovery.

Contribution—Sharing of a loss or payment among two or more parties.

Contributory Negligence—The act or omission amounting to want of ordinary care on the part of the complaining party which, concurring with the defendant's negligence, is the proximate cause of his or her injury.

Coroner—The public official whose responsibility it is to investigate the circumstances and causes of deaths which occur within his or her jurisdiction.

Costs—A sum payable by the losing party to the successful party for his or her expenses in prosecuting or defending a case.

Counterclaims—Counterdemands made by a respondent in his or her favor against a claimant. They are not mere answers or denials of the claimant's allegation.

Court—The branch of government responsible for the resolution of disputes arising under the laws of the government.

Cross-claim—Claim litigated by co-defendants or co-plaintiffs, against each other, and not against a party on the opposing side of the litigation.

Cross-Examination—The questioning of a witness by someone other than the one who called the witness to the stand concerning matters about which the witness testified during direct examination.

Custodial Care—Nonskilled, personal care, such as assistance with activities of daily living.

Damages—In general, damages refers to monetary compensation which the law awards to one who has been injured by the actions of another, such as in the case of tortious conduct or breach of contractual obligations.

Decedent—A deceased person.

Defendant—In a civil proceeding, the party responding to the complaint.

Defense—Opposition to the truth or validity of the plaintiff's claims.

Dehydration—Condition whereby a person's loss of bodily fluid exceeds his or her fluid intake.

Delirium—A mix of short-term problems with focusing or shifting attention, being confused and not being aware of one's surroundings.

Dementia—The irreversible deterioration of mental faculties.

Deposition—A method of pretrial discovery which consists of a statement of a witness under oath, taken in question and answer form as it would be in court, with opportunity given to the adversary to be present and cross-examine.

Discovery—Modern pretrial procedure by which one party gains information held by another party.

Duty—The obligation, to which the law will give recognition and effect, to conform to a particular standard of conduct toward another.

Edema—Excessive accumulation of water in the tissues.

Elder Law—Laws regarding the rights of elderly people.

Elopement—The ability of a nursing home resident who is not capable of self-preservation to successfully leave the nursing home unsupervised and undetected and enter into a harmful situation.

Expert Witness—A witness who has special knowledge about a certain subject, upon which he or she will testify, which knowledge is not normally possessed by the average person.

Eyewitness—A person who can testify about a matter because of his or her own presence at the time of the event.

Fact Finder—In a judicial or administrative proceeding, the person, or group of persons, that has the responsibility of determining the acts relevant to decide a controversy.

Finding—Decisions made by the court on issues of fact or law.

Foreseeability—A concept used to limit the liability of a party for the consequences of his acts to consequences that are within the scope of a foreseeable risk.

General Damages—General damages are those damages directly referable to the breach or tortious act and which can be readily proven to have been sustained, and for which the injured party should be compensated as a matter of right.

Gerontology—The study of the elderly and the aging process.

Gross Negligence—The intentional failure to meet the required standard of care in reckless disregard of the consequences to another.

Guardian—A person who is entrusted with the management of the property and/or person of another who is incapable, due to age or incapacity, to administer their own affairs.

Health Care Provider—An individual or facility licensed to provide health care.

Hospice—A facility where the terminally ill are provided care and comfort.

Implied Consent—Consent which is manifested by signs, actions or facts, or by inaction or silence, which raises a presumption that consent has been given.

Incapacity—Incapacity is a defense to breach of contract which refers to a lack of legal, physical or intellectual power to enter into a contract.

Infancy—The state of a person who is under the age of legal majority.

Informed Consent—The requirement that a patient be apprised of the nature and risks of a medical procedure before the physician can validly claim exemption from liability for battery, or from responsibility for medical complications.

Injury—Any damage done to another's person, rights, reputation or property.

Inspection Report—Written findings that support a federal or state determination that a nursing home failed to meet certain federal regulations or state requirements.

Intentional Tort—A tort or wrong perpetrated by one who intends to do that which the law has declared wrong, as contrasted with negligence in which the tortfeasor fails to exercise that degree of care in doing what is otherwise permissible.

Judgment—A judgment is a final determination by a court of law concerning the rights of the parties to a lawsuit.

Jurisdiction—The power to hear and determine a case.

Jury—A group of individuals summoned to decide the facts in issue in a lawsuit.

Jury Trial—A trial during which the evidence is presented to a jury so that they can determine the issues of fact, and render a verdict based upon the law as it applies to their findings of fact.

Lay Witness—Any witness not testifying as an expert witness.

Legal Capacity—Referring to the legal capacity to sue, it is the requirement that a person bringing the lawsuit have a sound mind, be of lawful age, and be under no restraint or legal disability.

Long-Term Care Ombudsman—An independent advocate for nursing home residents.

Malfeasance—The commission of a wrongful act.

Malnutrition—A serious health problem caused by poor nutrition.

Medicaid—A joint Federal and State program that helps with medical costs for people with low incomes and limited resources.

Medical Malpractice—The failure of a physician to exercise that degree of skill and learning commonly applied under all the circumstances in the community by the average prudent reputable professional in the same field.

Medicare—The Federal health insurance program for people 65 years of age or older.

Mental Abuse—The intentional infliction of anguish, degradation, fear, or distress through verbal or nonverbal acts.

Minor—A person who has not yet reached the age of legal competence, which is designated as 18 in most states.

Misfeasance—Improper performance of a lawful act.

Neglect—Referring to a nursing home resident, the failure to provide a resident with the proper care needed to avoid harm or illness.

Negligence—The failure to exercise the degree of care which a reasonable person would exercise given the same circumstances.

Negligence Per Se—Conduct, whether of action or omission, which may be declared and treated as negligence without any argument or proof as to the particular surrounding circumstances, because it is contrary to the law.

Non Obstante Verdicto (N.O.V.)—Latin for "notwithstanding the verdict." It refers to a judgment of the court which reverses the jury's verdict, based on the judge's determination that the verdict has no basis in law or is unsupported by the facts.

Nursing Home—A residential facility that gives nursing care or custodial care to an ill or injured person.

Nursing Home Abuse—The infliction of physical pain or injury on a nursing home resident by a person having care or custody over the resident.

Nursing Home Negligence—The failure to exercise the requisite standard of care in connection with the treatment and supervision of a nursing home resident.

Nursing Home Reform Act of 1987—Federal law governing nursing homes which gives nursing home residents certain rights.

Objection—The process by which it is asserted that a particular question, or piece of evidence, is improper, and it is requested that the court rule upon the objectionable matter.

Pain and Suffering—Refers to damages recoverable against a wrongdoer which include physical or mental suffering.

Parens Patriae—Latin for "parent of his country." Refers to the role of the state as guardian of legally disabled individuals.

Parties—The disputants.

Physical Abuse—The intentional use of physical force that results in bodily injury or pain.

Plaintiff—In a civil proceeding, the one who initially brings the lawsuit.

Plan of Care—Refers to the comprehensive individualized care plan for residents required under the Nursing Home Reform Act of 1987.

Pleadings—Refers to plaintiff's complaint which sets forth the facts of the cause of action, and defendant's answer which sets forth the responses and defenses to the allegations contained in the complaint.

Power of Attorney—A legal document authorizing another to act on one's behalf.

Prima Facie Case—A case which is sufficient on its face, being supported by at least the requisite minimum of evidence, and being free from palpable defects.

Proximate Cause—That which, in a natural and continuous sequence, unbroken by any efficient intervening cause, produces injury, and without which the result would not have occurred.

Punitive Damages—Compensation in excess of compensatory damages which serves as a form of punishment to the wrongdoer who has exhibited malicious and willful misconduct.

Quality Improvement Organizations—Groups of practicing doctors and other health care experts that are paid by the Federal government to check and improve the care given to Medicare patients.

Question of Fact—The fact in dispute which is the province of the trier of fact, i.e. the judge or jury, to decide.

Question of Law—The question of law which is the province of the judge to decide.

Release—A document signed by one party, releasing claims he or she may have against another party, usually as part of a settlement agreement.

Relief—The remedies afforded a complainant by the court.

Res Ipsa Loquitur—Literally, "the thing speaks for itself." Refers to an evidentiary rule which provides that negligence may be inferred from the fact that an accident occurred when such an occurrence would not ordinarily have happened in the absence of negligence, the cause of the occurrence was within the exclusive control of the defendant, and the plaintiff was in no way at fault.

Restraints—Any method or device designed to restrict the movement of one's body.

Retainer Agreement—A contract between an attorney and the client stating the nature of the services to be rendered and the cost of the litigation.

Service of Process—The delivery of legal court documents, such as a complaint, to the defendant.

Settlement—An agreement by the parties to a dispute on a resolution of the claims, usually requiring some mutual action, such as payment of money in consideration of a release of claims.

Sexual Abuse—Nonconsensual sexual contact.

Skilled Nursing Care—A level of care that must be provided or supervised by a registered nurse.

Skilled Nursing Facility—A nursing facility with a staff and equipment able to give skilled nursing care.

Summons—A mandate requiring the appearance of the defendant in an action under penalty of having judgment entered against him for failure to do so.

Survival Statute—A statute that preserves for a decedent's estate a cause of action for infliction of pain and suffering and related damages suffered up to the moment of death.

Testimony—The sworn statement make by a witness in a judicial proceeding.

Tort—A private or civil wrong or injury, other than breach of contract, for which the court will provide a remedy in the form of an action for damages.

Tortfeasor—A wrongdoer.

Tortious Conduct—Wrongful conduct, whether of act or omission, of such a character as to subject the actor to liability under the law of torts.

Trial—The judicial procedure whereby disputes are determined based on the presentation of issues of law and fact. Issues of fact are decided by the trier of fact, either the judge or jury, and issues of law are decided by the judge.

Trial Court—The court of original jurisdiction over a particular matter.

Undue Influence—Abuse of position of trust in order to induce a person to do or refrain from doing something.

Venue—The proper place for trial of a lawsuit.

Verdict—The definitive answer given by the jury to the court concerning the matters of fact committed to the jury for their deliberation and determination.

Verification—The confirmation of the authenticity of a document, such as an affidavit.

Vicarious Liability—In tort law, refers to the liability assessed against one party due to the actions of another party.

Ward—A person over whom a guardian is appointed to manage his or her affairs.

Wrongful Death Action—An action brought to recover damages for the death of a person caused by the wrongful act or neglect of another.

Wrongful Death Statute—A statute that creates a cause of action for any wrongful act, neglect, or default that causes death.

BIBLIOGRAPHY AND SUGGESTED READING

The Administration on Aging (Date Visited: June 2003)
<http://www.aoa.gov/>.

The American Association of Retired Persons (AARP) (Date Visited: June 2003)
<http://www.aarp.org/>.

The American Board of Medical Specialties (Date Visited: June 2003)
<http://www.abms.org/>.

The American Geriatrics Society (Date Visited: June 2003)
<http://www.americangeriatrics.org/>.

The American Medical Association (Date Visited: June 2003)
<http://www.ama-assn.org/>.

The Association for the Protection of the Elderly (Date Visited: June 2003)
<http://www.apeape.org/>.

The Association for Responsible Medicine (Date Visited: June 2003)
<http://www.a-r-m.org/>.

Black's Law Dictionary, Fifth Edition. St. Paul, MN: West Publishing
Company, 1979.

Center for Medicare Advocacy (Date Visited: June 2003)
<http://www.medicareadvocacy.org/>.

The Centers for Medicare & Medicaid Services (Date Visited: June 2003)
<http://www.medicare.gov/>.

The Elder Abuse Prevention Information & Resource Guide (Date Visited:
June 2003) <http://www.oaktrees.org/elder/>.

The Federation of State Medical Boards (Date Visited: June 2003)
<http://www.fsmb.org/>.

Health Care Choices (Date Visited: June 2003)
<http://www. healthcarechoices.org/>.

The Hospice Patient's Alliance (Date Visited: June 2003)
<http://www.hospicepatients.org/>.

The Joint Commission on Accreditation of Healthcare Organizations (JCAHO) (Date Visited: June 2003) <http://www.jcaho.org/>.

Medical Review Foundation, Inc. (Date Visited: June 2003) <http://www. malpracticeexperts.com/>.

The Medicare Rights Center (Date Visited: June 2003) <http://www. medicarerights.org/>.

The National Citizens' Coalition for Nursing Home Reform (Date Visited: June 2003) <http://www.nccnhr.org/>.

The National Health Law Program (Date Visited: June 2003) <http://www. healthlaw.org/>.

The National Institute on Aging (Date Visited: June 2003) <http://www. nia.nih.gov/>.

The National Senior Citizen Law Center (Date Visited: June 2003) <http://www. nsclc.org/>.

Nursing Home Info (Date Visited: June 2003) <http://www. nursinghomeinfo.com/>.

Social Security Administration (Date Visited: June 2003) <http://www. ssa.gov/>.

U.S. Department of Health (Date Visited: June 2003) <http://www. dhhs.gov/>.

United States Department of Health and Human Services Office of Disability, Aging and Long-Term Care (Date Visited: June 2003) <http://aspe.os.dhhs.gov/daltcp/home/>.